The Man behind the Mask

The Man behind the Mask

The Journey of an Orthopaedic Surgeon

Thomas H. Mallory, M.D.

University of Missouri Press
Columbia and London

Library of Congress Cataloging-in-Publication Data

Mallory, Thomas H., 1939–
   The man behind the mask : the journey of an orthopaedic surgeon / by Thomas
H. Mallory.
        p. ; cm.
   ISBN 978-0-8262-1773-8 (alk. paper)
   1. Mallory, Thomas H., 1939–   2. Orthopedists—United States—Biography.
I. Title.
   [DNLM: 1. Mallory, Thomas H., 1939–   2. Orthopedics—United States—
Personal Narratives.   WZ 100 M255 2007]
   RD728.M35A3 2007
   617.4'7092—dc22
   [B]   2007028907

Designer: Stephanie Foley
Typesetter: BookComp, Inc.
Printer and binder: Thomson-Shore, Inc.
Typeface: Simoncini Garamond

Frontispiece: Coat of arms by Joanne B. Adams, BFA, CMI. All illustrations by
Joanne B. Adams are reproduced courtesy of Joint Implant Surgeons, Inc.

To Kelly, all my love, all my life

Contents

Preface

Donning a surgical mask before entering the operating room has long been a surgeon's preparatory ritual. The mask serves to protect the health and well-being of both patient and surgeon during invasive procedures. Most masks conceal a person's identity, but the surgeon's mask offers no such protection beyond the operating room. Some might say that physicians wear an invisible mask as they interact with patients from day to day, a facade constructed to shield themselves from psychological involvement with the patient's condition. While this perception is not unusual, it can be explained as a product of the objective and calculating realism learned from the scientism during medical education. The physician is trained to be a technocrat, to solve a physical problem irrespective of the emotions and persona of the human being suffering that problem. In the process, physicians often lose the ability to express themselves or interact in a manner that touches the psyche. They allow expertise to subvert emotional expression, but this might well be a result, a response to the stresses and strains inherent in the job they have undertaken as a life calling.

As I write these memoirs, I hope to dispel the myth that surgeons are emotionally invulnerable or cold, untouched by the humanity of the patients who entrust them with their care. I can say that it was indeed tempting to construct a protective shield around myself when I was dealing with patients, especially in reaction to the mistrust and accusations of those patients who brought malpractice lawsuits against me. However, I understood that the doctor-patient relationship was an essential part of my practice as a physician, and this understanding may have set me apart from other practitioners.

In these memoirs, I hope to share the human perspective of a surgeon's life and recount some of the joys and sorrows, blessings and disappointments that I experienced throughout my career in medicine. I hope to identify the inborn and inbred qualities that prepared me for the rigors of medical training. I describe the impressions and opportunities that directed me on the path to become an orthopaedic surgeon, and I recount the slow and difficult process of shifting a medical paradigm in a field entrenched in tradition. After a period of success, I have now experienced the loss of my own health, and I describe the great burden I felt with a Parkinson's disease diagnosis before I discovered the true blessings and freedoms its passage has brought into my life. My discovery of painting has given me a true release from the role of surgeon in which I had been so utterly absorbed for so many years. I am thankful for the opportunity to express myself aesthetically in a way I might not have known without the disease that changed my life's course.

The story of my life you are about to read recounts a journey truly unplanned and unscheduled. My reacting and enacting were always in a spirit of adventure, anticipation, and actualization. I have learned from many mentors, colleagues, students, patients, and friends. I am indebted to those who have encouraged me to write these memoirs, and most important I am infinitely grateful for the love of my life, my most cherished wife, Kelly. I am indebted to many for their efforts to make the publishing of this book a reality. I especially appreciate the work of journalist Diane Morton, MS, of Jackie Russell, RN, of Barbara Lutes, and of various colleagues, including Dr. Seth Greenwald.

Part 1

An Endless Education

CHAPTER 1

How It All Began

It all begins at home.

This journey of a lifetime all began in late October 1954 when I was injured in a high school football game in rural Ohio. A sophomore playing defense on the varsity squad, I incurred a blow to my left knee, which resulted in an "unhappy triad" (torn meniscus, anterior cruciate ligament, and medial collateral ligament). Several months later, I underwent surgery at the White Cross Hospital in Columbus, Ohio, where I noticed all the young interns dressed in white coats. "What would it be like to be one of them?" I wondered. I remember this as being the start of my interest in the medical field. The more I thought about the profession, the more fascinated I became.

I am the second of three sons born to Guy and Freda Mallory. My father and my mother infused us boys with vision; they wanted us to excel beyond what they had achieved. My parents were schoolteachers, and although their economic means were small they were able to make much out of nothing. We three Mallory brothers became known for our athletic interest, our work ethic, and our sense of responsibility and industry. I vividly remember my father repeating to us how important it was for his boys to be manly, to choose a profession in life that built integrity and respect and that reflected good citizenship. Much of this discussion in my teenage years stemmed from a statement made to him by the legendary football coach Ara Parseghian.

My brother Bill, four years my senior, was an outstanding football player in high school and was recruited to play football at Miami University of Ohio under Coach Parseghian. When my father took Bill

3

to the university to begin his college career, Coach Parseghian told him: "Mr. Mallory, you bring me a boy. I'll send you a man." This statement so impressed my father, I remember him telling my mother about it when he returned home, and he repeated it often to my younger brother, David, and me as we struggled to understand exactly what was expected of us. So, what is a man?

Well, by my father's definition, as well as Coach Parseghian's and brother Bill's, it meant being tough, persistent, and avoiding at any cost the label of "wimp." When conflict or controversy arose, a man would "suck it up," play tough, not complain. A man was aggressive, but also reasonable and compassionate, with few words and few tears. Brother Bill displayed these qualities in a genuine way and even to this day is a quiet, tough, enduring individual. He fulfilled my parents' expectations while setting the pace for David and me. Bill went on to become a successful Big Ten college football coach at Indiana University and several other Division I universities. He is a national speaker, a committed family man, and a mentor to me.

I thought the pursuit of a career in the medical profession would qualify in my parents' expectations, and I considered the benefits: I would be helping others, while gaining respect and financial security and enjoying an exciting, challenging life. I reviewed my academic capabilities: I was a good student, not particularly strong in math, but I had an enviable capacity to memorize data, and I was keenly interested in science. Now I needed the personal experience factor to be sure.

So I went to the community hospital in Hillsboro, Ohio, and told a nurse: "I think I want to be a doctor." She suggested I could perhaps be an orderly, and I became the first high school student to work in the hospital. I spent many days there delivering direct patient care. I was responsible for a six-man ward every Saturday morning, giving baths, changing beds, assisting with the wound-dressing changes, taking care of ancillary needs, taking time to visit with the patients. I developed an interest in the doctor-patient relationship and began working on my communication skills. I began to see into the reality of this profession. Some people got better, some people died. I observed the biology of wound healing, the symptoms of infection, the look of the chronically ill patient, the value of patient support, the constant need for a caring environment. I enjoyed this work; it was a job with a purpose.

When school was out for the summer and most of my peers were baling hay or doing other farmwork, I took a job at the hospital working five days a week. It was during this time that I experienced the operating room for the first time. A local surgeon who had trained at the Mayo Clinic in Rochester, Minnesota, allowed me to look in on his surgery. We developed a great relationship over time as he sensed that my interest was deep rooted and genuine. He gave me many of his general surgery textbooks, and I enjoyed going through them, looking at the pictures of various exposures, noticing the position of the instruments and their uses, realizing there was a methodology to this science. I was fascinated by anatomy, how different techniques controlled bleeding or allowed entrance into and exit from the human body, and the ability of the body to recover. I was compelled but at the same time confused by some of the events I witnessed. Surgery was not always consistent. It seemed to progress well at times and poorly at others. The surgeon had a bad tremor, which made it technically difficult for him to operate, but he was competent and continued serving the community in a valuable way.

The operating room continued to fascinate me. I even began to visualize it according to a football paradigm, where the surgeon was the quarterback and the foe was the illness. A team huddled around the quarterback as he operated the event. A tension existed between the foes. As in any athletic encounter, there was a mission to accomplish. The team members made their preparations, executed their steps, handled any resistance or difficulty, and this all culminated in a final decision. Sometimes the match was easy, sometimes it was hard. Eventually I began to visualize myself as a player. I would need a coach, a team, and a game plan. I would need to evaluate the reasons for a win or a loss and to keep a constant focus on winning.

I found another observation enlightening as well, and this was that not everyone has the capacity to do surgery. I enjoyed the grace of the surgery performed by the surgeon I watched, despite his tremor. Little was I to know at the time that one day I would also experience the same challenge. I noticed his gentle touch as he handled the tissues, and the adept way he controlled the bleeding. Tissue splitting and dissection, the dedication to pathology, the amount of support needed to achieve these actions, the teamwork, all these I found fascinating to watch. The anesthesiologist was responsible to keep the patient alive under stress; the scrub nurse had to remain in constant communication with the surgeon and be ready to support at any time. On the occasion a surgical first assistant attended, his role was to facilitate, stay out of the way, and create exposure for the surgeon to work. The surgery was a beautiful performance, and the patient was almost healed by the time the wound was closed.

It was a compelling experience, but I was aware even at this early stage that complications do occur after surgery and this bothered me greatly. I made the vow that, if I became a surgeon, I would attempt to avoid such complications. The surgeon's manner outside the operating room varied. It seemed to me that the therapeutic persona was missing in his demeanor. He seemed distant and formal, and the doctor-patient relationship was strained. He seemed in a hurry, a bit impatient, arrogant, and not very cordial. I perceived that the patients had to have an intuitive sense, on their own, as to whether they were getting better. I promised myself I would try to be more involved in the doctor-patient relationship, more of a partner in a shared experience.

All these impressions built a practical foundation before I graduated from high school in the spring of 1957. I was preparing for my college education at Miami University of Ohio. I had the good fortune to be offered an all-inclusive scholarship to play football.

CHAPTER 2

Miami University, Oxford, Ohio, 1957–1961

Education is the best provision for the journey to old age. —*Aristotle*

I entered Miami University in Oxford, Ohio, in the fall of 1957, committed to pursue an undergraduate degree in preparation for medical school. This meant I had to decide whether to major in chemistry or in zoology, and I chose zoology because I did not particularly like chemistry. The basic courses in physiology and zoology were comprehensive, and I found them fascinating. They were extensions of classes I had completed in high school, which included also the dissection of frogs and other reptiles. During these sessions it became apparent, even to me, that I had a tactile dexterity for dissection. I could dissect specimens with speed and accuracy, to the point that upon a few select occasions I was even asked to present my dissections to fellow students. My anatomy professor once said to me during dissection of a frog, "Maybe you'll be a surgeon some day." I remember responding, "I want to try."

I found the professors at Miami to be stimulating. They made the curriculum interesting, came to class well prepared, were knowledgeable of their subjects, and appeared to have a genuine interest in the premedical students. The zoology curriculum was interspersed with occasional opportunities to deviate, and I greatly enjoyed the elective courses because they offered relief from the awesome burden of memorizing and analyzing scientific data. Philosophy, sociology, theology, English, literature, and psychology opened for me an opportunity to ask the question of the person, who abounds in the person, and what humanitarian dynamics would entail. In these classes I recalled the many discussions I had shared with my father during my teenage years concerning humanistic philosophy, including doctrine of the classic philosophers Plato and Aristotle and the oriental philosopher Lin Yu Tang. The university subjects were demanding in all facets, and the academic pace and competition among students intense. I felt intellectually challenged as I gained confidence in my ability to handle the topics included in the premed education curriculum. My freshman year progressed well, my grades were good, and my enjoyment of the zoology courses was obvious.

On the football field I experienced a different level of play, but this arena instilled in me values that later helped me endure the grueling mental challenges of medical school, residency, and long arduous days in the operating room (see Figure 1). Football promoted a philosophy of life that taught the players to be tough at all times, to be confident, to take over, manage, motivate, and achieve. Football was not academic or intellectual, it was physical. It prompted ruggedness and perseverance in the face of intense fatigue or pain. I was undersized for a college football player, and I took some huge hits. At times I was hit to the point of being crushed, which made me angry, and I realized that my response would either make me or break me. I developed a ferocious and tenacious spirit at my position and went on to be considered one of the most aggressive players on the team.

I discovered that playing college football had some perks. My poor vision required corrective lenses, for example, and although I hated to wear glasses, I could not see the ball without them. A trainer told me that if I made the varsity squad I was eligible to get contact lenses. So when I made the team, I went off to Cincinnati for contacts. This change of vision opened a whole new world to me—not only could I see the ball, I could see the players' numbers, and the players too!

In those years, all the football scholarship athletes were required to work in the cafeteria every night following football practice. Scholarships now do not carry this stipulation, and premed students generally do not play football. But it was a different era back then. Another premed student and I would leave the cafeteria and study late into the night in the furnace room of the dorm because it was the only quiet place we could find.

My sophomore year continued much the same way. It was challenging to play varsity football, work in the cafeteria, and study vigorously for the more complicated and difficult courses of general chemistry, organic chemistry, physics, and advanced zoology, which encompassed comparative anatomy. Chemistry remained a struggle for me, but I excelled in the zoology courses. My mind and general capacity were just not good

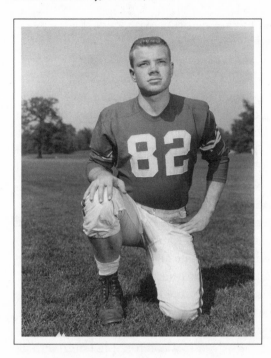

Figure 1.
Tom Mallory playing
football for Miami
University of Ohio.

in mathematics or the exact sciences but were better in the biological sciences. I learned to appreciate the anatomy and physiology of many systems. It was exciting to learn about the structure and function of the animal world and its relationship to human life.

Although my focus was more academic than athletic, I continued to enjoy football and the physical release and the alternative it provided to the intensity of studying. In November that year I was elevated from third to first string on the football team after injuries sidelined the first- and second-string players at my position. The big game of the year was homecoming against Bowling Green University, and I was designated to play left end. I was given the awesome responsibility of destroying the end sweep on defense. I was nervous. But as the game unfolded, my nervousness left me, and as my confidence grew I felt a sense of responsibility toward the team. Some years later a similar feeling and realization would recur as I worked in the operating room. The homecoming game actually went well. I played intensely and stopped some of the sweeps, though some proceeded around me, but what I remember most is the feeling I had of engagement, a sense of duty to a large group of people other than myself, and I found this a maturing experience. I felt a much larger and more adult individual at the end of the game.

My enjoyment of football and undergraduate course work was tempered with the thought that I would be applying to medical school amid stiff competition and with no means to pay for it. These concerns were always on my mind. The students at Miami who were striving to make it into medical school fell into three distinct categories: the truly smart, the smart, and the not too smart. I would have to say that at different times I fell into all three categories. The truth was that if I had the time and if I studied then I did quite well, but with football obligations and with working in the cafeteria I had continuous distractions. I managed to maintain my grades at an acceptable level. I remember the encouragement I received when a renowned surgeon from Cincinnati came to lecture to the premed students. He was well dressed and articulate and told us not to be intimidated by the competition but to remain earnest in our commitment.

There was no question I was committed, but I had serious concerns about the economics. How was I to pay for medical school? I had supportive parents, but they were people of low economic means. We had always had enough to eat, and we lived in a comfortable home with all the essentials, but there was never any extra. Nothing was acquired beyond what was actually needed. Education was encouraged and whatever funds were available were gladly given, but certainly my parents did not have enough to pay for me to go to medical school.

All I could do at that time was work to save as much money as possible. So I worked each summer for the county highway department. I worked on the bridge crew, hauling wood and steel to the guys who built bridges, or with the asphalt crew on road construction. I enjoyed working to make money. It seemed to me that my paycheck was a reward for my efforts, like a cold glass of water at the end of the long hot summer day, or the shower after a long hard workout, or the breath that gets restored after a long run. I worked all the time, either in the cafeteria during the school year or on the construction crew in the summer. So I developed a strong work ethic. It motivated me to become financially solvent and instilled within me a desire to become a responsible physician so that I would not have this constant concern about finances. I anticipated a life in which I would be married to a beautiful woman, live in a delightful home, drive a nice new car, have a house full of children, and live life well—the American dream.

This desire was reinforced often because, whenever mention was made that my career pursuit was medicine, I felt a sense of adulation from other students and adults. It made me feel glad to be about things that were worthwhile. I began to wonder more and more about my destiny and the providence of God and His nature. I actively pursued Christianity and other religions and philosophy. I deduced that my future would be the result of my own efforts; I was a free moral agent and I should rely on my own efficiency and capacity to resolve the challenges before me. The sense of God in my life was distant. I felt I was to create my own sense of integrity and morality, for I had no deep or abiding feeling that God could be involved in a personal relationship with a mere mortal such as myself. My spirituality was introspective and self-directed, and my relationships at school tended to be transient and superficial. My social affect was secondary, stifled by my educational commitment and the dedication I felt to my personal journey.

I mostly followed the football crowd and reflected the athletic, macho dynamic. The macho dynamic was especially challenged during the hot summer football practices. In those days, hydration was not considered a performance issue, so we took salt tablets and practiced without drinking a lot of water. I can still remember how dry my mouth would get; the ill effects of dehydration and extreme exertion would last for days. My body was so stiff and sore every morning that even getting out of bed and standing up was a challenge. Nonetheless, I returned to practice every day and endured the barbaric process.

During my junior year at Miami there was much discussion about preparing for application to medical school, which occurred during the spring semester. The application process involved taking an aptitude test, submitting a transcript for scrutiny, completing interviews, and most important, gaining the support of the local faculty. Outside activities were considered important; applicants were screened not only for academic capacity for the workload undertaken, but also for how they balanced the course work with a diversity of other activities. If a student's energies were too diluted, his educational capacities would falter, but it was imperative that everyone have something besides good grades on the application. I remember lamenting how much study time was lost while I devoted the necessary hours to football and work in the cafeteria, but I learned that the students who had no outside requirements did not score significantly better on the medical school entrance exams.

Miami University had an excellent record of placing students in medical school, and this was a definite advantage for me. The schools most popular with the Miami premed students were the University of Cincinnati, Ohio State University, and Case Western Reserve University. These medical schools were all within the state, reputable, and well established. Each school had liaisons working with Miami University professors, which thereby gave importance to the way students handled their personal relationships with their instructors and fellow students, and to the kind of impression they made. All aspects of the applicant were considered in determining the kind of practitioner a student would make in the world of medicine. I was not particularly outstanding in academics, but I was exceptionally competitive. I found that it made a big difference in my application that I had played football and experienced the rigors of a busy schedule. I hoped I would be accepted at Ohio State University.

Meanwhile it was the final season of my football career. I remember one game in particular, against the U.S. Military Academy at West Point, because it served as a pivotal time for me. It was October 1960, and we had flown into New York for the game on Saturday with plans to go into New York City to see the Rockettes perform on Saturday night. What a weekend this would be! On the first play of the game I made the kickoff tackle and promptly dislocated my elbow. I sat there in a haze of pain, thinking, "Not another injury!" I had sustained multiple injuries, concussions, and "slamming" throughout my football career, but I had never before felt such severe and stabbing pain. I could not return to the game and was forced to cheer from the sidelines, clutching my arm to my body while observing the nightmare. Miami lost the game badly, but I refused to give up the chance to see the Rockettes perform. I went to the show with my arm in a sling, gritting my teeth against the pain, but I was barely able to enjoy their much anticipated performance. When I returned home I had to be hospitalized because the pain and the swelling were so severe.

Although I enjoyed football, my heart and soul were no longer in it, and I walked away from that injury satisfied to leave any accolades of the game to my brothers. David, who had the greatest football talent in the Mallory family, was big like our father, standing well over six feet and weighing in excess of 250 pounds. On the field he was quick as a cat and deadly as a cobra. He had a real sense for the game and could be at the tackle point even before the play turned up the field. His talent attracted the professional football scouts, and he was recruited by the New York Giants and several Canadian football teams during his senior year at Miami. David was devoted to my father, so he listened when Dad told him, "Get a pro-fession and groom it because athletes have a season and there is no future." Dave went to dental school and then settled in a small rural community in northern Ohio to practice his profession for thirty years.

My football career was brief, but in retrospect I realize it was impor-tant in my maturation process, on my way to become a surgeon. I incurred several orthopaedic injuries that required surgery, which helped me view the procedure through the eyes of a patient, and often I wonder if my injuries influenced my decision to become an orthopaedic surgeon. Certainly I would not have been exposed to the medical world if it were not for my football injuries. I underwent a shoulder operation because of these injuries about the time I was accepted into medical school, and I remember specifically the acute pain and discomfort I endured. I had gained a sincere respect and appreciation for pain, and it was scary to think that I would inflict this kind of discomfort on people, even with the hope that I could make them feel better eventually.

So with football behind me, my focus now was devoted completely to gaining admittance to medical school. As the first semester of my junior year came to an end, medical school applications were being handled and decision letters sent, so acceptance and rejection was a common topic of conversation on campus. I talked with one of my bright friends who had been accepted at Ohio State University, and he told me he had met a secretary in the dean's office of the medical school who was informa-tive and knew exactly who was going to be accepted or rejected. He gave me her name and I called her on the phone to inquire about my appli-cation. "Competition is stiff and there are a lot of good candidates," she said. "Although your record is good, is there anything special about your situation that would make you a more attractive candidate than someone else?" I mumbled and fumbled for an answer, so she very kindly encour-aged me to visit the medical school and talk with some of the professors and the assistant dean.

With this in mind, I borrowed my friend's car and on a cold wintry day drove to Columbus. I met the informative secretary, and she imme-diately arranged for me to talk with several faculty members. I think they were impressed with my credentials and my persona, as they seemed to encourage me; in fact, I was surprised to find a few calls later that I was to meet with the dean of the medical school, Dr. Richard Meiling. He was an interesting man who had a military career and was very proper and formal in his manner. He asked me if I was a member of one of the alpha fraternities, and he expected an affirmative answer as he used various industries to measure capacity, social ability, and functionality. I answered that I was a member of the Beta Theta Pi fraternity and that I had played football for Miami University of Ohio. I told him I had had some very good experiences, but that I was a serious student and determined to become a physician at any price. I think my enthusiasm and purpose were evident to him, because I received an acceptance letter within a week of that visit. The letter stated that I was accepted into the Ohio State University College of Medicine, class of 1965. What an exciting time in my life! I had finally reached the point of no return; from here, I felt, there was no turning back.

Now my concern for financing became a very real issue. I applied for the Ohio State University Medical Rural Scholarship, an award given to a medical student who would return to practice in rural Ohio. I deemed myself eligible to apply because I anticipated becoming a general surgeon and returning to a rural community. I was one of five applicants called for an interview with the scholarship committee. During the interview I developed a rapport with those people and had a premonition that I would receive the award, which I did. The scholarship covered my tuition, which cost five hundred dollars per semester the first year. Unbeknownst to me at the time, my receipt of this award would become a point of contention with several people later, because I did not return to a rural community. (The issue was eventually resolved when I repaid the money for the scholarship.) My mother sent me one hundred dollars each month, half her monthly salary, to cover my living expenses.

As I reflect on these experiences, I realize how providence had opened opportunities before me, which later would be important on the journey to becoming a surgeon. These opportunities gave me a sense of responsibility to speak on my own behalf. I realized then—as I do now—that it is not so much the people you know but the people who know you that delineates the outcome. I also realized that the world measures people by where they belong, where they come from, and the kinds of relationships they have, a sort of family lineage. These may seem like phony criteria, but they continue to be used nonetheless.

I spent the summer before medical school at Bowling Green University in Bowling Green, Ohio, taking quantitative analysis, a difficult mathematic and chemistry course. I needed the course to qualify for admission into medical school. Alone and isolated, a long way from home and family, I realized I was losing the springtime of my life by going to medical school. I spent the evenings studying and then I would go out to run, which was when I would finally feel a sense of freedom and a release of tension. I began to focus on my passion for medicine, my desire to become a surgeon, which energized me to do whatever it took to reach that goal. I studied hard, managed to pass quantitative analysis, and was finally ready to begin medical school.

CHAPTER 3

The Ohio State University College of Medicine, 1961–1965

The direction in which education starts a man
will determine his future life. —Plato

I began one of the most rigorous endeavors of my life when medical school commenced with a convocation in Loving Hall at Ohio State University (OSU) in September 1961. The ceremony was a celebration of the opportunity before us, an achievement yet to be realized. All the professors paraded through the hall and the Hippocratic oath was presented. I remember particularly the pride with which the students wore their white coats and carried their little black bags once these had been distributed. Dean Richard Meiling addressed the entire medical class. Questions were asked, answers were given, but the ultimate questions remained. Who in the group would become a physician? Who would fail and be asked to leave medical school? Dean Meiling told us, "Some of you won't make it." All of the students asked within themselves, "Will that be me?" The journey on which we were about to embark seemed long, arduous, incomprehensible. We had a sense of anticipation and expectation, but there was a strong challenge before the class. In my heart I answered his question: "They'll have to tear me apart to keep me from finishing what I've started." I had quite a sense of accomplishment going; I had managed to get this far, and I knew, if I could do it to this point, then I was going to finish the course.

The rigors of medical school commenced immediately. Courses included gross anatomy, biology, histology, biochemistry, neurology, and others. The gross anatomy course was exciting for me, but not everyone shared my enthusiasm. The class was divided into groups with four students assigned

16

to each cadaver. I was placed with another male student and two women, an unusual distribution because there were only three women in the entire medical class. The women were bright but somewhat hesitant and the male student wanted to become a psychiatrist, so I was the only one of my group who enjoyed the dissections. As in undergraduate school anatomy classes, I had the dexterity to go through the tissues with speed, clarity, and confidence. I again was in a position to demonstrate various anatomy sites because of my ability. This confirmed my skill for this type of activity and served as a starting point for building competence in the arena of human surgery.

The hours spent in classrooms and laboratories were extensive, commencing at eight o'clock in the morning and finishing at five in the afternoon. After leaving the classroom I would eat dinner in the hospital cafeteria, and then be in my room ready to study by six o'clock. I studied intensively without a break until midnight, reviewing all my notes from lectures, reading the text assignments, and memorizing muscles, bones, and vessels. I was surprised at my dedication and ability to study. I found I could memorize continuously. Although I had studied hard at the undergraduate level, nothing consumed me so completely as my studies in freshman-year medical school. Around midnight I would finish studying, go to exercise, take a shower, and be in bed by one o'clock. I got up at seven o'clock, ate a quick breakfast, and was ready for class at eight. The male students dressed in shirt, tie, and the ubiquitous white coat even for class. Lunch at my apartment consisted of a sandwich and some milk. My lifestyle was simple, but I was driven by the thought that I was privileged to have the opportunity to become a physician, and no matter how hard I worked, someday I would be rewarded in a significant way. My freshman year was spent with book in hand, generally in the rooming house, far from the activities of any of my peers outside the medical sphere. I was spending the springtime of my life in pursuit of my goal, and I did not hesitate to pay the price. The vision of an exclusive, privileged process filled me with a sense of purpose.

The rapport I had with my classmates was interesting. We became fast friends. I learned how quickly relationships are built in intense situations. The stress was tremendous, and oftentimes we mutually would reinforce one other. Considering the amount of material we had to master, our vocabulary filled increasingly with medical jargon and terminology. We would get together on the weekends for study sessions and would study all day Saturday and Sunday. Friday evening was the only time I would take out of my study schedule to socialize. I did rather well in the first quarter considering the tremendous change in my life.

I remember a day during my freshman year when Dr. Robert Zollinger came to lecture to our medical class. He was the chairman of the department of general surgery and an OSU medical school graduate who had distinguished himself nationally and internationally as a premier surgeon. His manner was formal and he was impeccably dressed. His very presence commanded respect. Among his many accomplishments, he had been president of the American College of Surgeons and he had authored clinical textbooks and described and defined a condition known as the Zollinger-Ellison Syndrome. His demeanor was typical of the traditional general surgeon who had trained in the "old school," could operate on any area of the body, and had little respect for surgical specialties.

As I would discover in my clinical rotations later, Dr. Zollinger was treated like royalty. His statements were never questioned, as he pontificated about the life of a surgeon. Principally he emphasized the importance of an active life for a surgeon, and how difficult it was for many students to persevere through the education process. He outlined the fact that our education would go far beyond medical school; another four or five years of study would be required before any of us could become a surgeon. This time line seemed overwhelming to me. It was impossible to imagine how anyone could go on that long in the study mode. How old would a person finally be when they commenced to practice? And where would they get the money to live during this period of time? Yet Dr. Zollinger was a product of the very process he was describing. He seemed convincing. The question "Can it be done?" was answered by his very presence in our midst. I began to think about my life and how a third of it would be spent preparing for my life's work as a surgeon.

I was devoid of any awareness concerning the larger questions in life during this time. I remember one Friday afternoon, however, listening to a chant by a number of hippies who were marching down the center of the campus bellowing, "God is dead." For the first time in my life I realized that I really did not want to live in a world in which God was dead. I could not imagine a world without churches, temples, and mosques. I wanted to believe that a sacred and eternal persona existed in the universe. Even if God was dead in their opinion, I still was going to believe in Him, and perhaps my believing would make Him real in my life. The occasional trips to the Methodist church on the corner soothed my spiritual yearnings, but for the most part these were blunted by the intensity and focus of my pursuit. I was pouring out my energy every day to accomplish my pursuit, but it was not replaced with anything that would satisfy a spiritual need. I slept little, I exercised minimally, I ate poorly, and my social life was limited.

Occasionally a sense of craziness would overtake me, and I felt I had to break free from the bondage of this pursuit. I found a release only in the inebriated state induced by alcohol, and I began drinking excessively on Friday evenings. The binges and bashes became routine. I found myself anticipating these periods of release more and more. I would go to bed thoroughly intoxicated and wake up on Saturdays seriously hung over with an extreme headache, but I was fortunate that the headache would usually clear quickly and allow me to return to my studying.

When the first quarter ended, I went home to my little country town where my father and mother seemed so simple and plain, so innocent and naive, so puritanical. It seemed as if I had been a thousand miles away and in a different world. My high school girlfriend had found other moorings with a new friend. I returned to my school routine after Christmas break as if I had never been home. The winter and spring quarters went well with my accomplishments satisfactory.

One Friday night in the spring quarter, six of us medical students went together to a bar. I had several drinks and went outside for some fresh air. As I stood on the street corner, five teenage boys jumped me, hitting me from behind and knocking me to the ground. I tried to defend myself, but every time I swung at one of them, another would hit me. Here I was, a big football player being beaten by five pimple-faced kids. They hammered my face, and I heard one boy say, "Let's cut off his ear." One of them pulled out a knife and just then I heard a police siren. My assailants took off, and I looked up to see my five buddies just watching. They never tried to help me. The police arrived and I went to the emergency room at the hospital where they cleaned me up. It was about one o'clock in the morning by now. My face was hammered and my eyes were so swollen I could barely see.

The friend who had accompanied me to the hospital told me I had to have someone take care of me, and he offered to drive me home to Hillsboro. I resisted at first but finally submitted to the wisdom of his suggestion. I was mortified to knock on my parents' door about four o'clock in the morning, and then to face my mother when she saw me. I told her exactly what had happened, and by the look on her face I knew I had broken her heart. I went back to school the following Wednesday, deeply concerned about how far behind I would be in the course work. I began to doubt I would ever make it. To think I might fail in my pursuit because of the events of one evening spent in a bar drinking was a serious breach in my sense of morality. Although I continued to use alcohol for relaxation, I never forgot the moral sensitivity I developed when I thought of my behavior that evening. I remember distinctly my conviction that a doctor did not have the right to act in such an irresponsible way, and especially my conviction that I never wanted my friends or family to behold me in an inebriated state.

Later in the quarter I received a bad grade in biochemistry. The professor called me in to his office and told me that if I did not improve my grade I would flunk the class, which would end my medical school education. I went into the courtyard, sat down on a bench, hung my head, and asked God to help me pass biochemistry. I vowed that if He would do this for me, I would believe in Him earnestly. I passed the course with one of the top grades in the class. After this particular occasion, I began to consider the whole aspect of God very seriously indeed. I had made a deal with Him, and He met His obligation. Now it was my turn.

As the spring quarter came to a close, I began looking in earnest for a summer job that would not only give me money to live on but also be beneficial to my education. Several job opportunities came up, and one I pursued with enthusiasm was to work as a surgical technician in the operating room. An upperclassman advised me, however, that I really should spend the summer preparing for the sophomore-year pathology course, because success in that class was imperative if I expected to graduate from medical school. I decided to take a laboratory job in anatomy, which proved very easy to do because the research projects were mostly nominal and the work perfunctory. This job allowed a good amount of time for learning and reviewing the pathology materials I had obtained to study. I spent the afternoons reading ahead in the text and studying, then I could exercise and enjoy my student colleagues and frivolous activities in the evenings. The summer was passing by very quickly and then I found myself in a most unusual situation.

My encounters with women typically had been very superficial and brief. I believed I did not have the time for any serious relationships. I maintained a "here today, gone tomorrow" attitude, living for the moment. Relationships did not matter to me because the most important thing for me at that time was to get through medical school. This was the prevailing principle. That summer I had a number of casual dates, however, and then it seemed that the name Kelly Smith was coming up rather frequently. She was liked by many of her friends who attended nursing school. One day I decided to call her for a blind date. I knew the minute I saw her that I had encountered a most unusual and beautiful young lady. I immediately went into a tailspin. We were together every day, and within a few months we were very much in love. This created a problem for me, as I did not see how I could continue our relationship with the demands of the upcoming sophomore year. Kelly was in her senior year of nurse's training. Even though the timing was wrong, I could see no other possible relationship for us but marriage. We had made a commitment to one another, and we felt that we ought to have our love enshrined in marriage.

We both came from families of minimal economic circumstances, and it seemed logical to get married during the holiday break between Christmas and New Year's Day in a simple ceremony. We believed we would be much better off together than separated by our classrooms and activities, so we married on December 31, 1962. The marriage was a delightful affair in Lima, a little town in midwest Ohio. The minister was a kindly man and blessed us with the beatitudes and good wishes. We left Lima in a blinding snowstorm, to drive all the way to Columbus on our wedding night. My bride and I were wrapped in blankets because the 1946 Ford I drove had no heater and no defrost. I had my window open so I could wipe the windshield with my hand enough to see the road. What usually would have been a mere two-hour drive took much longer because of the road conditions. The following day we watched the Rose Bowl with Kelly's parents because we had no money to celebrate in any other way.

We started our married life in a little apartment on the third floor of a building where the bathroom was a floor below. We had old furniture and young spirits. To undertake marriage with the brevity of our courtship and our lack of funds was precarious, but I am forever thankful for divine providence because our marriage has been a happy and successful union for more than forty years as I write these memoirs. Kelly has always been the apple of my eye and we have loved one another immensely. She has been a dedicated mother, an exemplary wife, and has the capacity to continue to mature, change, adjust, advise, support, encourage, and provoke, all the time and at every instance with my interest and our interest at the forefront of her mind.

My primary academic concern during my sophomore year was to pass pathology. This was an enormous course. It not only covered the various organ systems, physiology, and anatomy, it also described and required a high level of understanding of the disease processes affecting every region of the body. This course was intense, indeed brutal, with extensive lectures that ended with long hours spent looking at slides of diseases, various stages in the disease process, and development of the effects of trauma and injury. At this point a few students admitted defeat and turned in their pathology books. What made the subject most challenging was the professor, who believed that the pathology course should be used to separate "the men from the boys." In his view, if you passed this course you had the right stuff to become a physician. His philosophy for the course was that "if you don't make a student do what he can't do, he'll never learn what he can do." The attrition rate was high, and 5 to 10 percent of the class would fail. Anyone who failed the practical exam then had to face the professor in a one-on-one oral exam. Those who failed had the chance later to repeat the course, or they were washed out of medical school and ended despite all their previous academics.

I studied endlessly and with luck kept passing the tests. The winter quarter passed by, as did the spring. Finals came, and I avoided standing before the professor by answering the questions in an appropriate fashion. I enjoyed the success of passing the exam despite the fact that I was extremely nervous. I remember walking out of the building that day in the spring of 1963, heady with the satisfaction that I was on my way to becoming a physician. What lay ahead of me now was the excitement and anticipation of clinical experience, wearing the white coat, walking the hospital halls, visiting the patients as I participated in their treatment.

Meanwhile Kelly finished her nurse's training and obtained a position in a local hospital. She worked that summer as a scrub nurse, but the hours and salary were terrible, and with both of us being on call we rarely saw each other. She sought a regular job and was fortunate to find a position at the university as a research nurse for a premier professor at OSU, a hematologist in the department of internal medicine. She enjoyed the job and kept it for all the time I was in medical school. She was on campus, and we would see one another frequently. We were looked on as a perfect couple, a team, working together toward my education. Kelly sacrificed any future educational and intellectual aspirations of her own in order to support my education, our marriage, and our family, and for that I shall be eternally grateful.

Our financial situation continued to concern me. Although my tuition was covered by the Ohio Rural Medical Scholarship, we needed help covering our living expenses. There was a county engineer in my home area, a prosperous farmer who had received his civil engineering education and was a county commissioner as well as the county engineer, who was known for his generosity. He had already sponsored several local young people and supported their education. So I presented my situation to him. I explained my desire to be a doctor, my lack of resources, and the finances needed for the educational process. He was very kind to me and receptive of my request, and I incurred a loan for what seemed at the time an enormous sum of money. He formulated a payoff proposal to take place after I finished medical school, and the interest was very modest. Finally, with the benevolence of this good man and with the Ohio Medical Rural Scholarship, I was financially solvent.

The larger picture of my indebtedness filled me with fear. I worried continually about whether I would be able to repay the debt and whether this obligation would limit my future educational opportunities. Little did I know that my financial situation would be a life-long seesaw. I would experience periods of affluence intermixed with indebtedness and risk. I would constantly be trying to build a balance between business and medicine, and constantly fighting the urge to spend in order to relieve stress. The proper and sensible use of money was a continuous struggle. Fortunately, my Christian faith greatly helped my financial management skills, once I realized that money was not necessarily something I was producing but, rather, something I was blessed to receive.

For the summer between my sophomore and junior years, I worked at the hospital adjacent to the state school for the mentally retarded. I worked with the medical staff, helping with the various needs that arose in these children. It was here that I was given my first opportunity to work in the surgical arena. The surgeon had trained under Dr. Zollinger at OSU and was a very nice person, extremely well trained, comfortable, and confident. He allowed me to assist in some procedures quite minor in nature but that were utterly engaging for me. The reverence I felt was as if I was in a temple or a church. The surgical act was delicate, the bone and tissue masterfully organized, and every time I touched the inside of a body it affected me in a spiritual dimension. I saw how much I did not know, how much I could perhaps learn to know, and I wondered if my education could take me to a point of surgical excellence.

The medical students were on call for the hospital, and I remember answering a call one night from a nurse who reported a child had a fever of 108°F. As a house officer I had learned that the most important thing for me to do was to use the telephone and follow the chain of command. I called the pediatrician and described the situation to him. He instructed me to give the child an ice enema, then to call him back. I struggled with that directive, not wanting to do something so drastic and inhumane to a child. But nevertheless, I followed the order and directed the floor nurse to proceed. Approximately thirty minutes later I called the nurse, and she stated that following the enema the child's temperature had dropped to 94°F. I called the pediatrician again and relayed the drop in the child's temperature, and he stated, "Good job." I did not feel completely comfortable, however. On reflection I concluded that although we had treated the symptom we had ignored the cause. Unfortunately I would encounter this same practice again in the future, a practice of symptom management rather than of defining causation.

The summer passed quickly, and I enjoyed the tasks of drawing blood, repairing lacerations, doing spinal taps, and performing tracheotomies for maintenance airways. The frequency with which I performed these tasks at the children's hospital helped to build my confidence. Yet still I was overwhelmed with feelings that I was working on holy ground, and that I still had so much to learn.

The junior and senior years of medical school were spent in medical and surgical specialties at various hospitals observing, studying, and caring for patients in many areas of the health-care paradigm. As medical students we were ranked as almost-doctors. We were insulated by the hierarchy and kept at the periphery, in positions that did not merit much respect. Indeed, the role of the student in the clinical years of medical school is undefined: your significance is almost transparent, you are so much the neophyte that you are a mere observer rather than a participant. The more confidence you develop as time seasons you, the more involved you become; but because you are only a medical student, you remain the odd finger on the busy hand.

I was amazed at the difference in teaching skills and capacities of the different medical faculty members. The best teachers were those who made the material exciting, who were committed to their role and interested in medical student education. They were informative, inquisitive, curious, articulate, and open-minded. Yet they were single-minded, compassionate, and stimulating. Then there were just as many who were not good teachers. They marginalized the medical students and minimalized their importance. They spent little or no time teaching the neophyte because their divided interest lay in hospital politics. I could see an established hierarchy, and I knew that in time I would reach that higher level. I also would have to endure the discomfort of the maturation process, including failure, criticism, and recovery. I was exposed to this process during medical school only to reencounter it as an orthopaedic resident.

The medical world within the hospital was a whole new arena. I was invigorated by the experience of seeing patients. We had many drugs to learn as well as the time, amounts, and methods of their administration. We evaluated the sick patient and tried to read the symptoms and signs observed in various areas of the body that would point to a particular diagnosis. The presence of Dr. Zollinger gave us a great advantage at OSU, for we received a tremendous surgical education, which continued to kindle my enthusiasm for a career in surgery.

It seemed at the time as if I wanted to specialize in whatever service I was on, from obstetrics to general medicine to surgery. These were basic rotations, and although the medical students played a minor role in the health-care delivery, we had responsibilities in each rotation that fell under the category of "scut work." These tasks consisted primarily of procuring X-rays, recording medical information, and performing minimally invasive maneuvers such as drawing blood, collecting urine specimens, and occasionally doing a spinal tap. The purpose of these rotations was to expose us to the processes of the health-care delivery system in the hospital, allowing us the opportunity to manage and organize ourselves according to the hospital agenda and format, and to engage in the doctor-patient relationship. Finally, and most importantly, these rotations allowed us to participate in a preceptor-type relationship with a senior colleague, where the patterns of practice are demonstrated and illustrated vividly every day.

I found the general medicine rotation to be enlightening as I was given the opportunity to see a process of diagnosis and treatment interplay in the hospital setting. I witnessed the effects of treatment on disease and the recovery process as it influenced the mind of the patient. However, the most exciting service for me was general surgery. This service allowed the surgeon to correct, alleviate, and adjust health conditions through invasive procedures. The general surgeon's primary venue is abdominal surgery; however, the training is all-inclusive and the general surgeon is capable of working in other areas of the body with some degree of familiarity. Although I did not fully appreciate it at the time, the basic general surgery education taught in the OSU medical school in those years gave the medical students an extremely good preparation. The general surgery residents trained in all areas of surgical specialties, including thoracic surgery, orthopaedic surgery, neurosurgery, urological surgery, plastics, and even obstetrics and gynecological surgery. This broad threshold of exposure allowed the residents to make choices. They could pursue a surgical specialty or continue with general surgery.

What I found most interesting about the general surgeons I encountered was the caliber of their personalities. They were impressive. They exuded self-confidence, were excellent technicians, and interwove their knowledge and understanding of bedside medicine with the surgical procedure. But one could also understand how the general surgeon might come to be just too general, for no one could truly master every area of the body. The complete and thorough mastery of each area of surgery lay in many years of study, preparation, and repetition.

It was during my junior year that I began to moonlight to earn more money and to ease some of the financial pressures I felt because of our lack of funds. A medical student could work in a hospital under the direction of a licensed physician and make a wage of four or five dollars an hour. Although this type of activity was frowned upon when carried to excess, I enjoyed working in receiving rooms, working on the floors, starting intravenous lines, and helping with emergencies. It was enjoyable work and very beneficial to my training.

Another dimension to the work was to develop my skills of communication. I felt I had been called to medicine because I really wanted to help alleviate the pain and suffering of humanity. During the years of moonlighting, which I continued throughout my residency, I found I had the capacity and the personality to provide therapeutic listening to patients. Finding a listening ear seemed to comfort them. I liked to befriend them and tell them as much as possible to make them comfortable, and develop a sense of humor and rapport that was invigorating. I interacted well with the nurses, students, and physicians and became quite popular with this crowd. I very much enjoyed these early years.

During this time I also had several opportunities to get into the operating room and begin to test the waters for real. The senior year was different because now the medical students selected the surgical specialty that interested them. My choice was orthopaedic surgery.

During my senior year I was also elected president of the senior medical class. I am not certain how this happened. I do not remember campaigning for the office, but somehow I found myself placed in this position of great honor. I had the exciting opportunity to serve as a representative of the senior class, to meet administration, spend time with the dean, and learn how to adjust socially with the affluent medical societies. It was a trial by fire because I had to learn how to dress and how to act in this exclusive arena. I received invitations to attend events with prestigious talent, and to frequent dining halls and private clubs such as the Columbus Club. This was a different facet of the socialization of the medical student and medicine. Another responsibility of the senior class president was to maintain class unity. We all became very close as we realized our times together were coming to an end. Once we started the next phase of our graduate education, many of us would need to say goodbye, maybe forever, as the momentum of medicine in our lives and careers would send us into new and different venues.

At this time the senior medical students were finalizing and securing internship opportunities to bridge the year between medical school graduation and the beginning of residency. The internship year was an opportunity to be fully licensed and qualified as a physician while continuing to learn in a structured environment. I accepted an internship with a first-rate private hospital in Columbus.

Graduation day dawned bright and sunny in June 1965. The ceremony was held in the famous OSU football stadium known as the Horseshoe. I had been there many times for football games when the stadium was filled with more than ninety thousand fans, but on this day the graduates and their families occupied just one small corner of the stadium. It was a special day for me. Mom and Dad attended, along with Kelly and her parents. I felt very proud wearing my hood and gown with green draping, symbolizing academic achievement from the Ohio State University College of Medicine. I had a real sense of accomplishment for completing a long journey, and finally I had acquired the degree I sought and would carry with me for the rest of my life. The diploma I held in my hand signified my successful effort to date. I experienced a moment of sudden joyous affirmation, realizing I had a skill that, when fused with a God-given purpose, truly would make me a physician. I was a young man with a future. I had bought it with years of sweat and effort. Although I have graduated from various other programs and exercises in my life, no experience has equaled or surpassed graduation day from medical school.

In the back of my mind I acknowledged that I still had a long road to travel before I could be considered a polished physician. On graduation day I made a commitment to pursue a path that would merit the effort I had expended to date, a path toward more experience, professionalism, competence, kindness, and compassion. These qualities were exercised in the next phases of my education: internship and residency.

CHAPTER 4

Orthopaedic Residency, 1966–1969

It takes a long time to find a shorter way. —*Anonymous*

Social conflict in the 1960s and the Vietnam War affected my life in many ways, but I was fortunate that none of these forces derailed my pursuit of the goal I had chosen for my life. I had to deal with the realities of the draft and my sense of duty to my country, but unlike many of the doctors who were siphoned off to war, I was offered choices that were beneficial to me both then and later. I received notification from the draft board in my county that I would be drafted if I had not secured a residency or enlisted with an army reserve unit by a specific date. I quickly assimilated myself into a reserve unit, the 2291st MASH Unit. Within a week I also received notification that I had been accepted into the orthopaedic residency program at Ohio State University.

My first residency rotation was the general surgery service. I would be under the direction of Dr. Robert Zollinger, the well-respected and renowned general surgeon, and an icon of the university. He was insistent above all on following the classic surgical education. He tolerated the sub-specialties of surgery, but his emphasis was on the classic traditions of general surgery.

I was fortunate to be diverted to the vascular surgery service under the direction of Dr. Sam Marable, a well-trained vascular surgeon. He was in his early forties, at the prime of his career, an excellent surgeon, a devoted family man, and a very kind and concerned individual. He always spoke quietly. In him I saw, for the first time, how important it is to be a good person in addition to being a good physician. He took great time with the residents, not only to teach the surgical skills and the diagnosis and treatment of disease but also to discuss the subtleties of medical practice such as billing, economics, how to handle the nonpaying patient, patient rapport, doctor-patient relationships, and nurse-physician relationships. I spent many long hours working with him over the operating room table. He was always genuine in his appreciation of the student doctors and of their potential for the future. Because the service was busy and the resident help was scarce, I was allowed to first-assist. I assisted in whatever way I could. I learned to tie knots very well, my hands were quick, and I learned to stay out of the surgeon's way. Dr. Marable was a staunch teacher, a firm disciplinarian, and an inspiring mentor.

It was during this rotation that our first son, Scott, was born. I will never forget the morning that Kelly and I went to the hospital together, she to the delivery room and I to a surgical case with Dr. Marable. During the case I was informed that I was the father of a bouncing baby boy and that my wife was doing well. I raced from the operating room to see her and the baby. She was radiantly beautiful and seemed utterly complete with Scott in her arms. Dr. Marable took the time out of his busy schedule to see her and the baby during his rounds.

Two years later it came as a stunning shock to me to learn that Dr. Marable had end-stage pancreatic cancer. One of the first-year residents asked me, "Did you hear about Marable?" I said, "No, what?" and the resident told me, "He's got cancer." I was numb with shock. I remember going to see him in his hospital room. I looked at him and I did not know what to say. All I remember hearing was the strains of "Bridge over Troubled Waters" as I encountered for the first time a physician as patient. He died a few weeks later, leaving behind a bereaved family. It was an absolute tragedy. I was beginning to appreciate the fragility of life, how there are no assurances, that even the most qualified of human beings must experience life's uncertainties.

After the three months of general surgery rotation, I was on anatomy rotation, teaching gross anatomy to medical students. Dr. Paul Curtis instituted teaching as part of our residency when he became chairman of the division, and I found this first encounter with teaching very enjoyable. I hoped I would continue to teach in whatever practice I eventually found myself. I had class myself in the morning, and then I taught in the afternoon. The leisurely, comfortable pace of the anatomy rotation was amenable to me as I was able to spend more time with my family. The birth of my first son had a profound effect on me, as I began to focus more on my relationship with my family, and my genuine commitment to my wife and son grew greatly during this period. Kelly and I had always enjoyed a good marriage, but something about the presence of children brought us closer together and deepened our love for one another.

The holiday season passed quickly, and I was soon engaged in neurosurgery, the busiest service I had ever experienced. Neurosurgeons are an interesting group of people. On a daily basis they deal with profound loss and with tragic and hopeless conditions. The neurosurgeons I encountered on this rotation were cynical, arrogant, and daring, all qualities that are required of a surgeon who is brave enough to operate on another person's brain and nervous system (which is a total enigma to me even to this day). We would stand for long hours as a surgeon would open the cranium, clear the blood vessels away, and enter the brain. The brain is such a mysterious area of the body, it was hard for me to fathom the audacity or courage required of a trained surgeon to enter this area.

Probably the most interesting and challenging portion of my neurosurgery residency rotation was the six weeks I spent in pediatric neurosurgery at a large general children's hospital affiliated with the university. This division of neurosurgery was harsh, intense, and exhausting. I remember the Sunday I went to take over the service. The resident I was relieving pulled an enormous pack of cards out of his pocket. There were between thirty-five and forty patients on the service at the time. On each card was written the name of a patient, a progress log, lab studies, and pertinent issues. The information on these cards was in considerable detail because of the complex nature of each patient's medical issues. The resident gave me the cards and said, "I'm out of here." He told me to give him a call if I had any questions, but essentially I was on my own.

I reflected on knowledge I had gained during my internship, which had taught me I could deal with a tremendous patient load only if I was really well organized. I had a naïveté based on my meager knowledge of neurosurgery, but with organization and a solid work ethic I effectively took good care of those patients. I went away from that rotation with a great deal of respect for the practitioner of this hard discipline, for in my view it seemed that rarely was any benefit gained on behalf of the patient. It would have been difficult for me to see any kind of positive reward in this specialty other than to comfort the patient who is suffering from neurological disease.

The spring—and last—quarter of my rotation year was spent in plastic surgery. I had been looking forward to this rotation because of the multidisciplinary crossover between plastic surgery and orthopaedic surgery.

Hand surgery, for example, was a domain dominated by either an orthopaedic surgeon trained in hands, a plastic surgeon trained in hands, or a general surgeon trained in hands.

The plastic surgery chairman at the time was a demanding individual, and he gave me a tough way to go, but his criticisms at that stage of my life were legitimate. Possibly the most valuable lesson I learned from him was the importance of reading the literature, especially if it was to be cited in a presentation or a publication. He had asked me to gather a list of references for a conference he was planning. I obtained the titles of several articles on the subject by copying the references out of a surgical textbook. He asked me if I had read the articles on my list, and I answered honestly that no, I hadn't. He gave me a scathing rebuke, stating that I should always read the papers I cited. It was a lesson I never forgot.

Another incident on the plastic surgery rotation that remains vivid in my memory is the time I treated a severely burned patient. He had developed pneumonia and needed an airway. At the time I was inexperienced at inserting tracheotomies, but the patient was in desperate need of one. It was a Sunday and I did not want to bother the chief, so I called an ear, nose, and throat (ENT) specialist, who confirmed the necessity for a tracheotomy and quickly performed it. The patient improved as the pneumonia resolved; the airway could be cleared, the lung capacity was improved, and the patient ventilated much better. The following day while making rounds with the plastic surgery chief, I encountered further criticism from him. As we entered a patient's room, he asked me, "Why does so and so have a tracheotomy?" I explained my reasoning and stated that the ENT service had performed the procedure. He told me angrily that I should never delegate patient responsibility. He insisted that, on his service, the residents would manage all crises as well as routine care.

I was extremely disappointed with his reaction. I believed I had made the best decision for optimum patient care, yet I was reprimanded because of turf wars between medical disciplines. It may have been a legitimate criticism that I did not discuss the issue with the senior staff physician, but I chose to proceed at my level of responsibility. It was another good lesson, and I never really forgot it as I dealt more and more with doctor-to-doctor relationships. I realized how important communication is in the decision-making process as well as in the continued relationships between colleagues. I never forgot that open and reliable communication is essential to good patient care.

My first year of residency was enlightening on many levels, and the wide range of different experiences broadened my surgical knowledge base before I commenced orthopaedic training. My initial exposure to the marvelous world of orthopaedic surgery was at the University Hospital in the general orthopaedic service ward. The year was 1967. I was well seasoned in crisis care and now was ready to learn reconstructive care in people with musculoskeletal disease.

I spent the first three months under the direction of the chief orthopaedic resident, Jerry McCloud, a most unusual individual with a remarkable aptitude. He had survived the arduous process of education under dire financial conditions with a wife and children. He was both clever and enterprising in his economic survival kit, working in various moonlighting jobs. He was a special fellow with a lot of self-confidence, an excellent surgeon who also enjoyed social encounters. Oftentimes together we would sign out of the hospital, cross the street to the local restaurant for lunch, then return to the care of our patients. On clinical or nonpay patients, Jerry had complete authority; he operated on them and was supervised at a distance by the attending staff. He in turn supervised the younger residents of which I was one. He assigned surgery to me that was both complex and difficult and then would lead me through it. I loved surgery. I loved the feeling of entering the body, correcting the wrong by doing something definitive (either applying a procedure or placing a prosthesis), then closing the wound, and watching the patient recover. We worked in every area of the body from the spine to the extremities. I was fascinated by this specialty that could make people better or at least more comfortable with their disease. So the decision I had made to pursue orthopaedic surgery continued to prevail. Unlike some rotations I had experienced, I continued to feel optimism as I worked in the musculoskeletal areas.

My second year of residency went by very quickly, and the cases I helped with were interesting. I remember assisting with a woman who had broken her hip in a fall and whose health was seriously compromised. It was questionable whether she could survive having an endoprosthesis placed into the femoral canal, but if the operation was to take place it had to occur rapidly. The chief resident called me and said that together we could do this operation, but we would have to practice the steps of the operation to ensure its success. We rehearsed it over and over and over again in the operating room, then we performed the surgery in less than one hour. We took care of the woman, she survived, and all was well. This operation was fascinating to me because we went from step to step in harmony without a word spoken between us. The unity between surgeon and assistant during this surgical procedure laid a foundation in my mind for what later was to become a way of life for me. At this time I really began to recognize the importance of methodology, of being organized in the operating room, and of knowing what resources are available.

My exposure to other practicing orthopaedists during my residency was enlightening. I watched all types from the young and aggressive to the old and staid. I did not witness any particular excellence or focused expertise, yet every operation was an adventure unto itself. The surgery was performed well, but I never felt like I was watching a master surgeon.

During this time, Kelly was pregnant with our second child. We rented an old brick home that was both pleasant and charming, located a short distance from the hospital. We stayed on that property for three years. The house was surrounded by green pastures, woods to walk in, a large yard for the kids to play in, and a big red barn with a horse in it. I came to realize how important it is to have a welcoming place to go at the end of the day, a place that is peaceful, restful, and renewing.

I was still moonlighting at various hospitals in the outer areas of the city for extra income, and I encountered several problems because this "employment opportunity" was discouraged. I was put on probation for working, but I believe it was because the medical school residency program intended to keep us pure. I do not regret the moonlighting experiences because they sowed seeds in my mind of effective patient care and patient communication that remained with me the rest of my days. Although it was a time of economic stress, I had a prevailing optimism that I was onto something that would reimburse and repay much of the indebtedness I was incurring.

I loved the morning conferences at the university, where fellow residents and I discussed the various topics of orthopaedics, presented particular patients and their problems, and listened to the comments of the experienced practitioners. Presenting the cases was stimulating for me, and I finally felt I was earning my rank. Despite my increasing experience, I recognized the boundaries to my function as a resident doctor. Some residents abused the privilege of the rigor and slow process of educating and developing surgical skills, but for every resident there comes a time when, no matter how well you are coached, you must go out on your own and apply what you have learned. The sooner you began to function independently, the further along in your development you would be.

I remember the first time I scrubbed with the chairman of the department. He was doing the simplest operation of transferring some tendons in an infant and he asked me to do part of the surgery. I was so nervous I started shaking. But then a calmness came over me similar to the time when I was given a starting role as an undergraduate on the football team at Miami University. I realized that this type of stress would always be a part of my life. Immediately the anxiety and nervousness left me, and I was able to perform the surgery efficiently and with confidence. As I gained experience I became more assertive and independent in the operating room. My surgery was considered good, and I knew it was.

Pediatric orthopaedics was a busy and interesting rotation, centered in the Children's Hospital. The pediatric clinics were enormous. The patients presented with cerebral palsy, spina bifida, trauma, foot and ankle deformity, skin problems, muscle problems, birth defects—a whole gamut of pathology. These children were cursed with weird and distorted maladies, yet they were young and spirited. I became aware that there exists a spiritual dimension to life that requires nurturing, even in the infant or small child, an inner source of strength that enables them to face their crises. These thoughts were comforting in the face of such severe challenges.

A typical day on the pediatric rotation was filled with a constant barrage of forearm fractures that little people so frequently sustain. The fracture "time zone" usually would run from two o'clock in the afternoon to early evening. On occasion I would have as many as twenty-five children with forearm fractures waiting for casting, and although I had to work at a brisk pace I thoroughly enjoyed it. I fell into a routine and could move quickly through the reduction and cast immobilization treatment.

The Children's Hospital portion of my residency was a happy time. Our second son, Bucky, was born. I remember the Christmas Eve that year when I was on call. I was anticipating a slow night, but late in the evening a fourteen-year-old girl was brought in with two fractured femurs. She had been out with her boyfriend and he wrapped the car around a light pole. I had to build a bed with ropes, strings, and weights for traction. Then I placed a pin in each tibia to hang the weights. It was a challenging job. I got home about seven o'clock in the morning on Christmas Day, and I sat in a daze watching the children enjoying their presents.

Meanwhile my military obligations were also enjoyable. I continued to attend summer camp and the weekend military retreats, which were actually a good experience for me as I aspired to proceed in orthopaedic surgery. The summer encampment in the MASH unit, part of the reserve army, was a welcome reprieve from the stress of residency training. The war was raging in Vietnam and much emphasis was placed upon recruiting and processing young men for military duty. The MASH unit of which I was a member was activated for two weeks during the latter part of June. The mission was to provide physical examinations for new recruits, with the idea that the process of induction could be enhanced by mass-producing the examination facilities. Our MASH unit was perfectly staffed for this particular mission: all the medical specialties were represented by the residents who had chosen to defer their military obligation while continuing their medical training.

Each summer we traipsed off to camp at Indian Town Gap near Harrisburg, Pennsylvania. The military camp had a long and distinguished history and reeked of military tradition, but despite the uniforms and the rank of captain I never felt a part of the military. My heart and passion were just not in that particular area, although I had great respect for the military organization and I met many committed and dedicated soldiers, both officers and noncommissioned members.

These encampments were periods of renewal and rest for me. I went back to my residency feeling rejuvenated, more engaged, and more committed than before. The army reserve experience underscored the importance of taking time off and changing pace. The break from residency restored my energy, and I discovered that renewed energy begets creativity, and creativity begets passion and purpose. I reconsidered my decision regarding orthopaedics. I knew it was possible to have a lifestyle in medicine that was quite casual, but that a casual lifestyle would not be found in the intense pursuit of excellence in orthopaedic surgery.

CHAPTER 5

Chief Resident,
1969–1970

The orthopaedic world is much larger than
Columbus, Ohio. —Paul Curtis, MD

My senior year as orthopaedic resident at Ohio State was a most significant time. I honestly believe now that everything preceding this year had been merely preliminary, and that this year served as the true entry level into the profession of medicine. As chief resident I began to assume supervised responsibility for the diagnosis, treatment, care, and ongoing management of patients. Heretofore I had always been directed, under observation, and limited in my capacities to exercise full patient care. Now I really was on my own, save for the scrutiny of the surrounding medical community consisting of the orthopaedic department chairman, the orthopaedic faculty, and my fellow residents. I felt I was truly on my own, because this position in a sense represented the real-life practice environment for the orthopaedic surgeon: I was accountable to my community, to my institution, to my profession, and most of all to my patients. Many memorable things happened during this year, and I will recall but a few.

As chief resident I was responsible for patients at the OSU clinic. A number of people came to this clinic each week. One of the first cases I remember was a gentleman who had a badly bowed knee. He was walking on a joint that essentially was bone on bone, so he had severe pain and could scarcely even get out of a chair. I had been reading the orthopaedic literature and believed he was a candidate for an osteotomy, a procedure in which the bone is cut below the joint and repositioned by shifting the weight-bearing center more laterally. I was enthusiastic about the procedure and truly felt it would help the man. He accepted my suggested treatment plan, and we proceeded to the operating room. I exposed the knee, cut the bone, and attempted to align it in the best manner possible. A large gap developed as I opened the wedge. We placed the deformed leg in a cast at the right attitude, anticipating that the bone would heal like any fracture. Postoperatively the patient had a protracted course of pain and discomfort, requiring frequent cast changes, and finally it became evident to me that the bone was not going to heal. I felt so sorry for the man; his deformity actually was worse than it had been prior to the surgery, and I acknowledged that I had provoked injury in a patient that worsened his condition instead of improving it.

A profound sense of responsibility overwhelmed me. I was filled with self-recriminations, but I began to self-talk and finally made a pledge that I would critique each complication, asking the questions as to what went wrong, what I could do to make it better, and how I could avoid a similar event in the future. A second surgery was required in which a bone graft was used at the osteotomy site. The bone graft went on to heal uneventfully; the patient gained a straight leg and finally was much improved. The whole scenario spanned the entire year that I was chief resident. I lay awake many nights thinking about this particular case. I began to ask myself serious questions. How can I be consistent as a surgeon? How can I provoke a response that is helpful? How can I be a better surgeon? Could I cut the bone in a way that it would not be traumatized but that would be therapeutic? There had to be a better answer for arthritis when the knee deteriorates beyond relief from medication and is mechanically defunct. Little did I know that someday I would have a marvelous answer for a patient such as this man. However, for my first encounter, both the patient and I suffered.

Many patients came onto our service through the emergency room, most commonly for fractures sustained in automobile accidents, or in the case of elderly patients, for broken hips. A broken hip usually was difficult to manage because of the fragility of the bone. The fracture could be treated in one of two ways: a pin and side plate could be placed across the fracture site or a prosthesis could be inserted after removing the fracture fragments. This prosthesis was inserted into the bone canal and would articulate within the socket portion of the hip. The surgery usually went well, but there were several precarious points in the operation involving the sciatic nerve, the major nerve sending motor impulses to the lower extremity. If the nerve was stretched, damaged, or injured at all, this was a catastrophic problem. The individual would be left with a flail dysfunctional lower extremity. I was fortunate to avoid this problem during my chief resident year but did encounter this complication later, in my private practice.

One patient who came in with a hip fracture had a remarkable experience. She was a demented woman who had fallen and broken her hip in a psychiatric hospital. She was sent to our hospital for treatment. She was wild with her affect. The attending surgeon took her to the operating room where the surgery went well. I was on rounds with him about ten o'clock that evening when he checked on her. She was sleeping and her condition seemed very stable. The next morning while we were making rounds, we came into her room and she was crazy, wild and screaming, "What did you do to me?" The surgeon told her she had undergone a hip operation and she yelled, "You put this thing in me!" She was holding the prosthesis in her hand. I almost fell over. She had literally dug it out of her hip. I could not imagine anything so gross. Yet he took her back to the operating room, and we cleaned her wound and put a new sterile prosthesis in place. After surgery we restrained her, and she proceeded to heal. As far as I know, she returned to her psychiatric confinement in a functional physical state.

As I reflect on this particular event, I am again reminded of the raw and painful human situations we face as physicians and surgeons. Experiences like this leave an agonizing impression, which can cause you eventually to become insensitive to some things you see and experience. On any given day a surgeon's experiences run the gamut—from the grandeur of an opportunity to help someone and see good results to the total opposite of that situation, either because of the circumstances of the nature of healing, misunderstood aspects of the patient's responsibility to be compliant, or the surgeon's competence.

Despite my best attempts to avoid them, infections would occur. I believe most could have been prevented with prophylactic antibiotics. At that time the use of preventative antibiotics was not condoned by the infectious disease consultants, however. They advised the surgeon not to start antibiotics until the bacteria in the wound was identified, and then a specific antibiotic, "the right drug for the right bug," could be instituted. Surgeons subsequently have learned that this is the wrong approach because once the wound becomes infected there are terrible burdens. Giving prophylactic antibiotics to the patient for the most common organism that could cause an infection preempts the start of infection.

I remember a senior surgeon requesting me to assist with a complex operation, and I agreed to help him. We performed a hip arthroplasty, and after the long and arduous operation I noticed the surgeon had written for prophylactic antibiotics to be given. He did not heed the advice of the infectious disease consultants who were suggesting no prophylaxis. I asked him about it, because of the instructions I had been given, and he responded, "Tom, I have learned that there are some things you do not question, you just do it and somehow it works." How right he was, but it took time to prove the real benefit of prophylactic antibiotics.

Meanwhile, this was my final year to gain surgical experience. If I did not learn during this year, I would not be prepared to practice on my own. I was selfish about the surgery, and because I did a lot of it myself I was not well received by my junior colleagues. The junior residents wanted to do the surgery too, and they were expecting me, the chief resident, to give them the opportunity to perform the surgery as I supervised. But that was not my game. I was there to learn to be a surgeon, and I knew I had to operate during this period in order to gain the necessary experience and skill to be the kind of expert surgeon I wanted to be. For the first time in my life I began to sense the intense jealousy and covetousness that often happens in the practice of medicine. I was self-focused, and arrogant, so my choices provoked reaction and I began to have problems with my fellow residents. I was considered to be "out for myself only," and in reality I was. The camaraderie I had enjoyed with my colleagues took second place to the pursuit of my own goals, so I was not the most popular person in the group.

This dissension spilled over into the conferences. Every week a general conference was held by the residents to present the surgery that had been performed during the past week. I presented my cases, explaining the diagnosis, the proposed solution, the surgical procedure, and the subsequent result. What a difficult time it was for me to be critiqued so judiciously. It was not that I did not want the criticism of the senior faculty, but it was the way in which it was delivered that affected me. They criticized my decisions in a way that left me very disturbed. But I am sure many were trying to point out the things they believed I had done incorrectly.

The chairman of the orthopaedic department was a perfectionist. He was a man well versed in the orthopaedic literature; he could turn every situation into a point-and-counterpoint. He introduced a concept to me that was intriguing, and true. He said the orthopaedic community is universal; it is not just a little conference room filled with doctors, but in a

sense the whole world watches. He conveyed that anything and everything we do as surgeons eventually rises to the surface, as the patient car-
ries that particular therapeutic event into the world. During the patient's
lifetime, he or she would encounter numerous others in the medical community so that eventually many practitioners would see my work in that
patient. One time he said to me, "You will learn, Dr. Mallory, that the
orthopaedic world is much larger than Columbus, Ohio." How true it
was, and I soon would learn about this world. I would seek an experience in the orthopaedic community. I would travel the world and become
a specialist in hip surgery. I would publish in the scientific literature. I
would find a world of medicine far beyond where I stood at that time
during my chief resident year.

In spite of challenging encounters, my senior resident year was pro-
gressing well until an incident occurred in the operating room that almost
ruined my career. I was the chief resident operating a spine case, and the
wound became quite bloody during the surgery. The operating team constantly consulted with the anesthesiologist to determine when the patient
was losing enough blood that transfusion was necessary. When the anesthesiologist ordered a unit of blood to be transfused, the circulating nurse
then would go to the blood bank refrigerator out in the hallway, choose
the blood package that matched the patient's blood type, and give it to
the anesthesiologist. The anesthesiologist then would hang the packet and
transfuse the blood into the patient through the intravenous line. If the
patient was losing a lot of blood quickly, there was only a small window
of opportunity to request the blood, to retrieve the blood package, and
to have it hanging at the appropriate moment. In this particular case, the
patient was small in stature with a respectively smaller blood volume. We
knew that if this patient bled excessively, the blood volume would deplete
quickly. This would require rapid transfusion to avoid surgical shock. In
this case, the circulating nurse in the surgical suite was very indifferent
to the situation, not the least bit affected or impressed by any young surgeons rotating through her operating room. She had seen hundreds of
them and respected only the most senior surgeons.

So she ignored me when I asked her to obtain blood that day; she was
too busy talking with another person in the room. I could hear them talking about some trivial issue when the anesthesiologist again reported that
the patient needed blood. I asked the nurse again to please get a unit of
blood for us. I went back to operating and five or ten minutes passed.
When I looked up again, she had not yet left the room, and I asked again,

this time in a loud voice, to get a unit of blood for this patient. Her response to me was "You don't talk to me that way. I will do it when I want to." I felt something snap in my mind. Here I was struggling to help this patient whose life was in my hands, and matters were getting serious. I asked myself if I was going to take this, knowing that she had no idea of the patient's condition. I stepped back from the table, tore off my gloves, strode over to the nurse, grabbed her forcefully, shoved her out the door, and shouted at her to get the damn blood and bring it here as quickly as possible. Everyone in the OR was appalled; they could not believe that a surgeon had physically pushed someone out of the operating room, the head nurse no less, and into the hallway shouting the way I did. I scrubbed back in while she went and retrieved the blood. We finished the surgery, and as I left the OR afterward I observed a note on the wall that ordered me to the boss's office immediately. When I went into his office, he said to me, "Your behavior in the operating room was inexcusable. You are fired."

I stood there in shock. Fired? You mean I have gone to school for four years of undergraduate work, four years of medical school, four years as resident in orthopaedic surgery, not including internship year, and here I am at the age of thirty-three years and I have been fired! What am I going to do? A myriad of thoughts ran through my mind as I left the office, the main one being that I could not practice orthopaedic surgery because I did not finish my orthopaedic residency. I knew I did not want to be a general practitioner. I was dumbfounded. I walked blindly to my locker, and as I removed my white coat, a profound sense of sadness came over me. I felt desperate as I drove home and knocked on the door of my house. I was so distraught I could not even turn the doorknob. My wife came to the door. It was early afternoon and I had never been home at this time. She had a puzzled look on her face as she opened the door and asked me, "What's wrong?" I said, "Kelly, I've been fired. I have lost my job, I have lost my position, it is over. What are we going to do?" The tears came to my eyes, we embraced, and then I saw my two little boys behind her. I wondered how they were ever going to survive. We sat on the chair and I told Kelly what had happened. We prayed that God would give us an opportunity to move past this time. I knew that what I had done was wrong, that I had been treated appropriately for inappropriate behavior, but even though the principle was wrong, the cause was right. I was upset with myself for having lost my cool, but I was upset that this nurse was allowed to be insubordinate, to continue to act the way she did, to be so indifferent to the needs of the patient. She was allowed to continue in the system and a person like me had to be fired.

As Kelly and I were sitting there, it was about half past four in the afternoon, the phone rang. It was the boss calling, and he asked that I return to the office to speak with him. So I got back in my car and returned to the hospital. By now it was about five o'clock. I went into his office to receive my sentence and he said, "I will reinstate you if you apologize to this nurse, but don't you ever, as long as you live, strike another nurse or anybody else in the operating room." I thanked him for allowing me to continue my education, and then I went to apologize to this woman for whom I had no respect. What was her response? I believe she realized she was wrong as well. Although I was able to return to my job, I believe this was an act of God. I was wrong, had reacted inappropriately, and had rightfully been relieved of my duties. However, I was given another chance, and I learned that I could not solve a problem by becoming part of the problem. I never will forget this particular experience; it will remain as one of the most memorable of my entire medical career. This is an example of the peer review process working to monitor physician behavior.

On the lighter side, the appearance of the senior orthopaedic practitioners caught my eye. Few made an effort to be attractive in terms of their style, attire, and manner. However, one stood out to me who more or less defied the white coat faceless image. He wore English tweeds with spats and vests, all neatly tailored and well groomed. He had a manner about him that was special, and I was extremely attracted to his style. He was a solid orthopaedic practitioner and took the time to care for veterans in the veterans' hospital system. One time he invited me to go with him to assist in a hip arthroplasty of a patient in the nearby community veterans' hospital. It was a bright and sunny day as he drove up in the most beautiful sports car I had ever seen. He was royally attired in his English tweeds. His entire persona presented just short of being eloquent. As we worked that day we discussed style, manner, and impressions. He reiterated that he felt there was something special about being a physician, and moreover he said you could lose yourself in the medical stereotypic roles. He chose to have his own individual style, and his patients noticed it, which he interpreted as a positive sign in terms of his encounters with them. He also explained to me how patients hold their doctor in high regard with a special respect and awe, and he said if I could individualize my style it would set me apart. The bottom line, of course, was being a good doctor and taking excellent care of the patient. But his comments impressed me. I already had decided that if I ever was to be affluent I would have a nice car, I would wear a tie and a tweed suit, and I would be well presented.

I had several opportunities to experience affluence with the residents' social agenda, which was strictly limited to the medical profession, with little opportunity for encounters with the extended family except for holidays. Kelly and I were invited to parties and other events that really were a mix of senior medical staff and current resident colleagues. At these events alcoholic beverages were abundant, and I could feel myself drifting closer and closer to a state of addiction at every event. It was perhaps because I was exhausted, and as in medical school these social events provided an opportunity to let down and release. I loved the elegant food, the comfortable affluence, the booze, the eloquent conversation; it was all an opportunity for sheer gluttony, pleasure, and enjoyment. I was sowing the seeds of an addiction for alcohol, and I knew I needed to come to terms with the problem before it increased to the point of destroying my career. I know I was not alone in this struggle. I believe many physicians have a tendency for addiction, whether for alcohol, drugs, work, sexual indulgences, or other forms of gluttony, because it serves as an avenue of release after extended periods of intense stress.

This exposure to abundance was in fact a sharp contrast to our daily existence. We had no money. We were living in utter poverty and were constantly borrowing to meet our daily living expenses. We had old cars, old clothes, old this, old that, and were finding no opportunity to alleviate increasing debt. I knew if I lived long enough I would be able to work my way out of this hole, and that I wanted to live well by worldly standards. I definitely was motivated to make money, because it was a necessity, to balance out the emotional and physical price I was paying.

One of the biggest topics of conversation for the senior residents was the formulation of their plans for going into practice after graduation. A fellow resident and friend, Henry Rocco, and I were discussing opening a practice together in a nearby Ohio college town. I felt very fortunate to have this opportunity to begin my practice, yet I was not sure I wanted to be a general orthopaedic surgeon.

However, I was certain I wanted to be a good surgeon. I wanted to operate well and know my subject, to walk with that special group of people who are recognized as the best. I knew I had a long grueling path ahead to achieve this designation. Model surgeons were well organized, quick in their surgical maneuvers, gentle in handling the wound. They had about them a sense of control and a relaxed alertness. They were leaders, and if you provoked them the whole wrath of God would come down upon you. They were in control of the operating room environment and elicited profound respect from others. Some characteristics of the model surgeon in this position were naturally endowed, but much was earned through discipline and experience, a regime that was essential for one to achieve the excellence of surgery.

As I contemplated my desire to strive for excellence, I saw an opportunity to broaden my horizons. A Harvard physician, Dr. William Harris, came to Columbus on the Michigan–Ohio State football weekend. He came a bit early to perform a cup arthroplasty. This was the operation of choice for arthritis of the hip prior to the introduction of total hip replacement. Dr. Harris was well-known for his expertise in cup arthroplasty. He brought his nurse and his instruments, and when he began to operate I knew I was finally watching a master surgeon. While we were at a party that evening, Dr. Harris suggested that I come to Boston for a fellowship in hip surgery at Harvard University. This opportunity excited me, but I was already verbally committed to joining my colleague and friend Henry Rocco in practice. What would it entail? I had no idea about a fellowship or taking another year of training and going to Boston. After I considered it, I thought perhaps it was a waste of time. Meanwhile, I talked to several of my colleagues and senior mentors and they agreed that a fellowship year would be redundant, that it probably would not do much for me as far as my interest in orthopaedic practice was concerned.

Kelly was very insistent that I pursue the opportunity, however, saying that the fellowship could be something I both needed and wanted. She thought it could make a tremendous difference in my medical practice if we went to Boston. After much consideration, we decided to apply for this Boston fellowship. The process was extensive and time-consuming, and we had little encouragement or direction from friends, family, or colleagues. Within a month I was notified that I had been accepted, and we quickly decided to go. I can say with certainty that the fellowship proved a pivotal moment in my life, and in culminating my journey of medical education.

One of the final surgical cases of my residency year was a cup arthroplasty in one of my clinic patients who had developed arthritis of the hip. The surgery was an absolute disaster. I spent hours looking for the hip joint, muddling in the entire problem. I could not determine the size or the position of the component, I could not reduce the hip or maintain stability. It was an eight-hour operation with extensive blood loss, and the poor man never did very well postoperatively. Little did I know that one day I would be able to perform a hip replacement operation in less than an hour, and that by the operation I could instantly change the lives of many patients. From the first step they took after surgery, they would have no hip pain. I was to enter an era where the expanding technology of artificial hip replacement was beyond imagination and the powers of reason. But this became reality as I opted for the opportunity to go to Boston.

As our senior year finished (see Figure 2), we attended banquets, celebrations, and tributes where each of the senior residents stood and expressed gratitude and thankfulness for their training and told where they had chosen to practice orthopaedic surgery in various communities and locations around the country. I was the only one of my class going off to take another year of training. It seemed foolish at the time, but I believed I was going on to something special. I wanted to be an extraordinary surgeon. I wanted to understand something so well that I would never question the appropriateness of what I was doing. I knew that to achieve this level, the Boston fellowship year was necessary.

Just as I was preparing to leave OSU for Boston, a tragic event occurred that affected me greatly as I considered the years I had dedicated to my education. I had become friends with a general surgery resident named Red over the four years of our residency. He was a lanky Iowa farm boy whose ambitions were to return to Iowa and practice general surgery in a small rural community. Red was considered a particularly good surgeon. He had a stellar reputation among the residents for his humility, his keen intellect, his dexterous capacity, and his genuine concern for others. He possessed spectacular skills in vascular surgery. I saw Red frequently in the hospital during our residency, and at all hours of the day and night. As chief resident of general surgery, Red would spend horrendous hours in the hospital looking after the sick and wounded. Late at night the emergency room would produce multiple trauma patients with vascular injuries and myriads of other problems. I encountered complicated vascular injuries in trauma cases with fracture of lower extremities that oftentimes required Red's utmost skill and training to manage. He and I often would be up all night taking care of these problems together. We shared life's aspirations as we worked. He was married to his high school sweetheart; they had four children, were utterly poverty stricken, and lived in a little shack around the corner from the hospital. Red kept talking about

Figure 2.
Tom Mallory at
graduation.

how life was going to be when he finally got into practice. He was going to have a nice big home, send his kids to a good school, continue to love and take care of his wife, and enjoy his hobby of quail hunting.

Prior to the completion of his residency, Red sent his wife and children to Iowa to look for a place to live, with plans to follow soon after. The last time I saw Red, his eyes were bright with hopes for the future, and his manner was quick and agile as he bid farewell to four arduous years as the house officer in one of the most difficult general surgery programs in the country. It really was a happy day as we shook hands and parted ways.

Shortly thereafter, I received a call from Red's wife, saying that he had been killed in an automobile accident. Apparently he fell asleep and drove off the road. I tried to comfort his widow and four children, but I was so taken aback by the tragedy, I do not believe I was much help at all. I ponder even to this day the awful irony. Red had studied and worked all those many years to become an accomplished surgeon, and then in one brief moment his life was wiped away. He never would know what he would miss or what he would gain. How quickly life can turn. Red was stopped before he could even get started. As I prepared for the Boston hip fellowship, I began to sense the process of attrition, and it took some steam out of my life's momentum.

I can say in retrospect that in the phases and stages of my maturation as a surgeon, I definitely had passed through the qualification process. I had gone to medical school and completed an orthopaedic residency. I had enjoyed a fulfilling senior year as a chief resident. I could now practice orthopaedic surgery safely, although I felt perhaps not skillfully, as the expertise I was seeking continued to remain elusive.

CHAPTER 6

The Hip Fellowship
in Boston, 1970

It is a mistake to try to look too far ahead. The chain of destiny
can only be grasped one link at a time. —Sir Winston Churchill

After I finished my residency in July 1970, I had just about one month
before I was due to report for my fellowship in hip surgery in the Harvard
health-care system. My mother and father hosted a small party for our
family to wish us well as we left for Boston. Then we pulled out of the
driveway and headed northeast in our two dilapidated old cars. Kelly
drove with Bucky, who was two years old, and I followed in the other car
with Scott, who was now three. Everything we owned in the world was
packed into those two cars as we began the two-day drive from Columbus
to Boston. The trip went well; we stayed at a motel that first evening and
had a nice dinner. We rose early the next morning to drive into Boston
that day.

In Boston we rented a suitable apartment. It was situated in Roxbury,
on the edge of an affluent suburban area, Chestnut Hill. The contrast
between the two areas was striking. Chestnut Hill was elegant; Roxbury
was a blue-collar community. A little creek ran along the back side of our
apartment building, and I often would take the boys to throw rocks in
the water and climb on the grounds.

Boston was intimidating, especially for a midwesterner such as myself,
yet I sensed something special about it, a spirit of adventure. I had a feeling I was on the edge of an invaluable experience. This destiny came to
life the first day of the fellowship, when I reported for morning rounds at
the hospital. I was told that morning rounds would commence promptly
at seven o'clock, and that I should be there ready for work. I arose early

that morning, because I was not exactly sure how to get to the hospital. I followed a route that took nearly an hour for me to locate the hospital. The traffic was fierce. As I walked up the front steps of the hospital, I had the feeling that I was on the verge of a life-changing experience.

The hospital was old but busy. Everyone spoke with a pronounced New England accent. I proceeded to the doctors' lounge where I was to meet my mentors and fellow colleagues. I met a senior fellow who had been there approximately six months; he was very pleasant and explained my responsibilities. Two fellows and one resident from the Massachusetts General Hospital program were on the service. The world-renowned surgeon Dr. Otto Aufranc soon would arrive to commence rounds. I had never met Dr. Aufranc, but I had already heard a lot about him. He was about sixty years old, a war surgeon who had returned to Boston and developed, along with his mentor, the cup arthroplasty operation. He now was world famous, and he had patients from all around the globe coming to him for this special hip operation.

When Dr. Aufranc entered the room, he shook my hand, welcomed me to Boston, and then commenced his rounds. He was a man of slight build with piercing eyes. His hands were small and delicate. He spoke in a very soft, low voice; I had to strain to hear what he was saying. He appeared a very humble person with a quiet, peaceful, gentle demeanor and yet a sense of strength about him. I thought this temperament unusual for a physician of his great fame.

After we walked into the first patient's room, I witnessed a phenomenon that to me was amazing, a doctor-patient relationship unlike any I had seen before. Between Dr. Aufranc and the patient emanated such love and concern, a palpable rapport between patient and doctor despite the patient's infirmity. The patients were usually in considerable pain immediately after the operation, because the metal cup moved against the bone and this was uncomfortable, but they received affirmation that it was worth the pain and suffering. Dr. Aufranc assured them that they soon would walk pain free. He sat on the edge of each patient's bed and quietly coached them through their physical therapy. He encouraged them when they hesitated to move their hip, relieving their tension so they could relax and their therapy could be performed without pain. I noticed immediately how healthy the wounds appeared; there was no swelling, the skin was supple and soft. Even the first day after surgery the wound appeared as if it had already healed. The patients responded well because Dr. Aufranc was viewed as the "perfect" surgeon. He was always upbeat, always knew exactly what he was talking about. He was a master at the bedside.

I clearly recall observing Dr. Aufranc operate. I had at last found the surgeon with the gentle touch, but with speed, definitive confidence, and complete knowledge of exactly where he was in the operation at all times. He knew where to begin and where to end, his dissections were clear and well-defined, all tissues were correctly planed. The incision and wound had minimal hemorrhage, minimal bruising and swelling. This was a beautiful operation performed by a great surgeon, and I gleaned all I could from this experience. It did not matter much to me that he never gave away any of his surgery; in fact it seemed that, if he did, he would contaminate or cloud the work he had already completed. He was a confident surgeon and was constantly in contact with the operating room environment, including the anesthesiologist, the scrub nurse, and his assistant. His eyesight was keen and his hands were strong. How did he reach this point of perfection? I asked this question frequently during my fellowship and I believe the answer rested in several elements. First and foremost he was an especially endowed individual, and second, he was well trained. The third reason was his experience; he knew every curve in the road. Finally, he was focused. His results were remarkable. This was a brutal operation, and it was amazing to me how well the patients did as I observed their postoperative course.

I enjoyed the many conversations I had with Dr. Aufranc during rounds, lunch, and time in the operating room. I consider him one of the greatest individuals I have ever had the honor to know, and I feel very fortunate to have been under his tutelage. He was kind and compassionate, and his soul was animated by a quiet spirit that was utterly committed to his beliefs. He had strict standards of performance that were difficult to compete against, even for the Boston elite. He was a man who inspired tremendous respect. People held him in awe, and certainly he was as polished and finished as anyone in the profession of medicine.

The operating room was Dr. Aufranc's realm of mastery. He positioned the patient appropriately for the surgery, and then he and his nurse draped the patient. The fellow seldom was allowed to help unless he was brought into the confidence of Dr. Aufranc. The surgery would commence and always progressed along the same pathway through the hip joint anatomy, with essentially a bloodless field at all times. Dr. Aufranc was a meticulous surgeon; I never knew whether the operation was hard or easy for him because it always appeared effortless. This observation was especially impressive to me, because when I was a resident my exposure to hip surgery had caused me to fear this operation. In my experience, the dissections were bloody and often I would get off track and wander around in the region of the hip looking for landmarks before I would get back into focus. None of this uncertainty was present with the Aufranc approach: it was direct, well disciplined, with an easy rhythm and synergy between Dr. Aufranc and his nurse, who had assisted him some twenty years. They had a silent communication between them as the operation unfolded.

Dr. Aufranc would attend his patients in a beautiful office, in an old brownstone edifice along Beacon Street near the Charles River. His patients were usually affluent, articulate, and well-established elderly people. He invited each new patient into the exam room and spent well over an hour examining them and reviewing the treatment options. He turned down a number of patients for surgery because of such issues as obesity, attitude, bone morphology, or any other reason it would not be in their best interest. He also had a number of patients coming in for their follow-up appointments, and he was very informative with them. He had an outlying program for their recovery, and he spent a lot of time explaining the exercises and how to distribute their body weight, how to walk, how to sit down, and how to get up from a chair. He personally demonstrated all of this to his patients.

Dr. Aufranc's office operated as efficiently and consistently as he did. His desk was always clean, he took care of all his dictation immediately and was always prompt with his correspondence. After office hours the fellow and the resident returned to the hospital to check the progress of the patients who had undergone surgery that day and reported their condition to Dr. Aufranc back at the office. In the evening hours, around eight o'clock, we would talk again about the patients' conditions. He operated two days each week, leaving three days to see patients, teach, and visit with his colleagues. He was an extraordinary teacher. He had a profound understanding of anatomy and an intuitive sense of how the body should heal in the presence of metal implants.

On a more personal note, Dr. Aufranc liked nice things. He drove a vintage Bentley automobile and had a special parking place at the hospital. He was a polished individual and always dressed in the same colors: dark blue suit, light blue shirt, and a maroon tie. The attire never changed. He was a very private person. He owned a stunning home in suburban Wellesley and had a beautiful wife and two sons.

I was Dr. Aufranc's last full-time fellow. He retired shortly after I finished my fellowship. It became obvious that he was in declining health by his weak and fragile appearance and manner. He developed myasthenia gravis, suffered terribly, and died within the next decade. He was a great one. I will always be indebted for his contribution to my education. He exuded excellence. He was a surgical artist, the perfect caregiver, and the consummate physician.

The fellowship had a more leisurely pace than any of the previous phases of my medical education. It was a practice of only hip surgery, which was an elective procedure, so the surgery occurred on a scheduled basis. We seldom had an emergency. The surgical procedures were completed in the morning, so once the patient was stabilized, my afternoons, evenings, and weekends were free. I had minimal night call, which left me with a lot of time to read and to observe other hip surgeons. Every morning I was in the operating room, watching surgery or to some degree participating.

I enjoyed the many advantages of living in Boston and experiencing the vibrant medical community. The weekly Grand Rounds at the Massachusetts General Hospital were stimulating, with many orthopaedic surgeons at all levels active there. The residents were bright, motivated, and highly competitive, but they were suspicious of the fellows and would frown upon a rotation that included them. They saw the fellows as intruding on their turf, and as for me, they had little time for a midwesterner with my educational profile. Their opinion really did not matter to me, though; I just went on my way and did my job at no one's expense but my own. I was very careful not to infringe upon others because I was there for only a short period as a trainee.

Around the hospital environment was a whole cadre of reconstructive hip surgeons, most of them emanating from the expertise of Dr. Aufranc. Everything stood in contrast to Dr. Aufranc. Drs. Rod Turner and William Harris were his junior partners, extremely energetic, ambitious, and entrepreneurial. They operated very efficiently, so they could manage a tremendous volume of surgery. They accepted the most treacherous and involved cases, attempting to model their patient care after Dr. Aufranc's methods. But Dr. Turner's energy and efforts went in several directions. He had a completely different philosophy in the operating room regarding the residents and fellows. He allowed them to do the surgery to a point of capacity, and when their capacity was reached, he expertly took over the operation. He introduced me to the mechanics of surgery. His aptitude was evident; he approached surgery from a mechanical rather than a biological standpoint. Whereas Dr. Aufranc nurtured the biology into a favorable response, Dr. Turner approached hip disease as a mechanical dysfunction that could be resolved with the use of a prosthetic device. It was Dr. Turner who first introduced me to the concept of total hip replacement (see Figure 3).

The development of total hip replacement had reached a point of proficiency that was quite remarkable. It was now possible to fix the prosthesis to the bone with an acrylic material called methylmethacrylate. This material would solidify and attach the device firmly to the bone. The patient then was able to bear weight almost immediately, which shortened the recovery after surgery. Many surgeons from the United States were traveling to Europe to learn the advancements in total hip replacement. Drs. Turner and Harris acquired a cement license, which was authorization from the Food and Drug Administration (FDA) that allowed them to use methylmethacrylate in a clinical study model. This license restricted the procedure to certain centers and to certain surgeons who were performing the early clinical trials evaluating the efficacy and safety of methylmethacrylate.

I was amazed at how quickly those with a total hip replacement recovered compared with those who had undergone cup arthroplasty. Patients who had cup arthroplasty required approximately six weeks to recover, and most of that time was spent in bed. However, the total hip patients were capable of getting out of bed within a few days. They usually stayed in the hospital for two or three weeks until the wound healed, but they were completely free of pain, and range of motion improved immediately. The contrast was remarkable.

Awareness of this operation was expanding within the Boston orthopaedic community. The operation was so successful that it became obvious to me over the next several months of my fellowship that more of these hip replacement procedures could and should be done. The name John Charnley kept recurring in conversation, and I began to seek out more information about this man. He was a British orthopaedic surgeon practicing near Manchester, England. He had established a hip center, a hospital used exclusively for this total hip operation, and he was performing four to six hip procedures a day. The center was a mark of efficiency and team effort. As my awareness of the efficacy of total hip replacement increased, I began to formulate a plan to visit Charnley when I finished my fellowship in Boston.

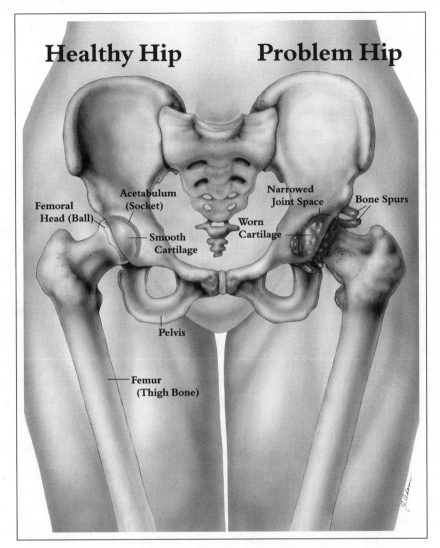

Figure 3. Illustration of the hip in a nonarthritic hip (left) and in a diseased hip (right). Note the loss of the joint space in the diseased hip. Drawing by Joanne B. Adams.

Meanwhile, I was learning as much as I could about hip surgery. A typical day consisted of either assisting Dr. Aufranc or helping other surgeons perform one or two operations, then spending the afternoon in the library reading about the methylmethacrylate cement, chrome-cobalt metals, polyethylene plastic, and the history and evolution of total joint replacement. This operation was going to change the face of orthopaedics and would become the surgical answer to the arthritic hip joint. I surmised that it could be an area of focus for my entire orthopaedic attention and that I could be sufficiently busy to maintain a practice exclusive to joint replacement. This operation would gain popularity, because Charnley in England had already proved its effectiveness. I believed that we in the United States soon would follow suit. This observation proved quite accurate, and centers were created, expertise was developed, and large volumes of hip replacement procedures were completed. I was fortunate enough to experience this development at the grassroots level.

Certain problems with the operation arose, however. A high risk of infection was inherent in the surgery, necessitating the use of prophylactic antibiotics, which still was frowned upon. The large amount of foreign materials used in the procedure justified use of these antibiotics to prevent infection. A second problem was the risk of prosthetic dislocation, and it became an increasingly frequent issue with the use of the posterior surgical approach. This problem prevails even today and is related to femoral head size, position, and muscle tension. It continues to plague this operation. Another emerging dilemma of the operation was prosthetic removal because of infection or component malposition, which could be quite difficult considering the hardness of the bone cement. Dr. Turner foresaw this problem and developed a method of extraction that would allow for removal of the device. It was not long before he began to receive a number of patients from all over the country, even the world, who needed to have their prosthesis revised for one reason or another.

Because of a growing awareness of the significance of this operation, I felt compelled to travel to England to visit Charnley and tour his hip center at Wrightington Hospital in Wigan near Manchester. By coincidence, Dr. William Harris's research team needed some information from Seth Greenwald, a young doctoral candidate from the United States studying in Oxford, England. Dr. Harris's research interest was topography of the hip, which involved the mapping of pressure points on the femoral head. New information from Greenwald's doctoral thesis on contact pressure in cadaver hips would be insightful in this regard. So Dr. Harris arranged to sponsor a trip to England for a few of his counterparts from the fellowship and resident group. I was fortunate enough to be selected, along with two other fellows, to go to England for a whirlwind four-day trip. We went to London to see Greenwald and to glean some of his information on hip topography. Then we went to Charnley's

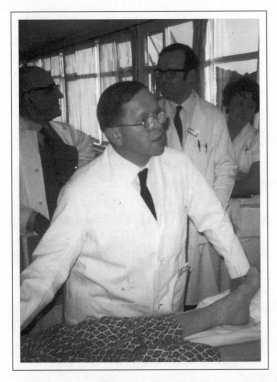

Figure 4.
Sir John Charnley.

hip center near Manchester for two days. This experience was one of the most inspiring experiences of my medical education, and the most important point was my encounter with John Charnley. He became one of my greatest heroes, along with Dr. Aufranc.

John Charnley was an unappreciated genius, the true master surgeon (see Figure 4). The concept of a hip center was unique, a hospital devoted entirely to the performance of hip replacement surgery and the postoperative care of these patients. Its success was obvious, as the world was beating a path to Charnley's doorstep. Both the patient and the practitioner were there for his expertise: the patient for the surgical procedure and the surgeon to learn the new technology. The technology involved the use of artificial implants fixed to bone with acrylic cement, which in application could function remarkably well. Both the patient and the practitioner were dazzled with the early results of the operation because no other reasonable alternative existed for managing the severe pain and discomfort frequently associated with arthritis of the hip.

For me the pilgrimage to the hip center was significant. I could not imagine starting a specialty practice in hip replacement without firsthand knowledge of what Charnley had created in his hip center. What I discovered was more than just a marvelous operation. I was introduced to a completely new method of patient management. For the first time I saw the importance of focus, the concentration of all efforts toward one particular therapeutic entity; the effect was one of complete concentration of effort in a specific direction.

To watch the operation being performed by Charnley was an experience unto itself. The surgery was done in a glass enclosure called a green house, a Charnley creation to prevent airborne contamination. The surgery was executed in silence; each step in the operation had been memorized and performed repeatedly. The surgery was divided into stages, and the set of instruments required for each stage was contained within a basket. As Charnley advanced to the next stage of the operation, a new basket of surgical instruments was passed and the instruments were removed from the basket and placed before him. He sat at a table-like structure with the patient in the supine position.

His surgical technique was straightforward. The whole operation took about one hour to perform. Absolutely nothing in the entire world could be likened to this operation. Its execution and its performance were light-years ahead of anything else going on in orthopaedics at that time.

It was difficult not to be overwhelmed by the execution of the operation, but the operation itself was only one part of the total system of care that commenced with the patient's admittance to the center. Before the operation the patients met with Charnley in a conference-like scenario. They were interviewed so they could be evaluated and graded according to a hip-scoring system. If they fell within a certain range, they were offered the surgery. The patients whose score did not qualify were placed on pain medication and asked to return in another year for reevaluation. Meanwhile those patients admitted to the hospital constituted some twenty-four cases a week performed at the center.

Charnley did not do all the surgery. He had consultants who performed surgery, and he also had registrars, who were orthopaedic residents learning total joint replacement surgery. The patients were managed primarily by nurse practitioners in large wards. The physicians monitored the care, but for the most part the patients followed a hands-off, get-well program. The patients recovered well, very few complications occurred, and those complications that did arise were addressed directly. However, the general routine was to let the patient progress through the system and, at the end of the program, be ambulatory with crutches and allowed to return home. Patients were seen on a yearly basis for follow-up, at which time hip scores were recalculated and the proof of success was documented by the absence of pain, the ability to walk without a limp, and evidence of walking endurance. The X-rays were scrutinized to determine if or where prosthetic component failure was occurring.

Literally hundreds of patients each year came to the hip center for their proposed total hip replacement operation. The efficiency with which the surgery was executed and the patient care given was quite remarkable. The organizational format predisposed the operation to be successful, and the success was such a consistent surgical phenomenon that the surgeon could plan a routine pattern of healing. I thought about this so-called clinical pathway and decided that, if I ever became established and had a significant number of patients, I definitely would pursue a clinical pathway management system. I was fortunate that this eventually did happen, and many of the patterns I instituted in my service owed their genesis to the systems I witnessed during my visit to Charnley's hip center in 1970.

Although not appreciated at the time, the contributions of John Charnley changed the face of orthopaedics worldwide. His innovation introduced the whole concept of subspecialization within the broad field of orthopaedic medicine and surgery. His contibution served as a stepping stone in the pursuit of excellence; the concept of subspecialization was valid, especially when there was an operation that was reproducible or predictable. Each patient was not a variant but instead fell into an established pattern. This pattern allowed for specific treatment modalities to be used during the course of healing and the outcomes were consistent and predictable.

As a result of the subspecialization or focus on one region of the body with a specific operation, the impact in orthopaedics was enormous. It seemed as though almost instantly the orthopaedic community segregated into a series of anatomical regions that produced special societies including one each for the hip, knee, shoulder, hand, spine, foot, and ankle. Heretofore, the world of orthopaedics had been one in which the practitioner roamed through the various regions of the body without specific focus or expertise. In those days, the definition of a "good" surgeon was one who did everything. But total joint replacement in Charnley fashion changed the face of orthopaedics. It created an expectation in the patient for a painless hip with normal function. Charnley created an environment where specialty care could be focused on the performance of the surgery, and boundaries of knowledge and information formed to ensure better activity and an operation level of excellence. Needless to say, Charnley greatly influenced my practice of total hip replacement, and I found it grievous when, some twenty years later, one of my residents asked me, "Who was Charnley?" I could not help but think how soon we are forgotten.

So I finished my fellowship year and entered the orthopaedic profession, still under the great influence of Drs. Aufranc, Turner, and Harris, and Professor Charnley. From Dr. Aufranc I learned the importance of a genuine doctor-patient relationship, and the value of educating and encouraging the patients through their surgical recovery. From Dr. Turner I appreciated the obvious reality that total hip replacement would usurp cup arthroplasty as the surgery of choice for the arthritic hip. From Dr. Harris I learned the importance of drive and determination. Finally, from Professor Charnley I learned the value of systems, from the initial patient office visit through the completion of the patient's therapy. Collectively, I could see the emergence of a health-care system associated with specific technology, and I set out to capture my observations in a format that could be used when I returned to Columbus. In the past, surgeons had always acted in an independent manner, at their own pace, and no formal or established clinical pathway was in place for the patient to follow through the health-care system.

I wanted to translate the Charnley system into a format that could be communicated and utilized in my practice. Much of the credit for the documentation of this system goes to Kelly, who worked endless hours taking my dictation and transferring it to paper using an old typewriter. We began first with the operation, breaking the surgery down into steps, which were defined in detail so that each operation could be done with a systematic approach. When variations occurred, the system was expanded to include the variation. We produced a protocol that described in detail the preoperative management, the steps to the operation including how to drape the patient and which instruments to use, and the postoperative management.

Next was a systematic pathway for communication with the persons supporting the surgeon, including the internist and the anesthesiologist. The internist had to be comfortable with the surgical patient and aware of the patient's surgical stress and the potential complications such as phlebitis and infection. The underlying health status had to be maximized prior to surgery, and areas of risk had to be identified. The anesthesia issue was a matter of conserving blood to avoid hypovolemia, or excessive blood loss. Use of bone cement could stimulate the peripheral system to bleed excessively, which could cause low blood pressure and a potential for cardiac arrest. Therefore, the surgeon not only had to be aware of the blood loss but also had to ensure that the anesthesiologist closely monitored the patient's volumetric state. The bottom line was that the operation itself must be supported by attention to these details, which protected and nurtured the patient.

As my fellowship drew to an end, I was offered the opportunity to remain in Boston and work with a group of orthopaedic surgeons as a junior associate in hip surgery. But Kelly and I were eager to get back to our home in Ohio, to be close to family as our children grew and started school. I decided to join two of my resident colleagues who were now practicing in Columbus. They had a thriving general orthopaedic practice. It seemed the right thing to do. At that time total joint replacement had not yet been performed in Columbus. I was confident that, once I had the opportunity to demonstrate hip replacement in Columbus, the operation would prove itself effective.

We left Boston with fond memories, great friendships, and a tremendous increase in optimism. The blessing of information and knowledge I had received was invaluable and never would have happened had we not gone to Boston. I had authenticated myself by going there and by working at Harvard. The experience broadened my awareness—from the orthopaedic knowledge needed in a small local community to that shared in national and international forums. My exposure to the world of orthopaedics during the fellowship left me with a feeling of fraternity with hip surgeons around the world who were developing new technologies.

My Boston colleagues hosted a big party for me when I left, which made me feel truly appreciated and honored. The director of the program gave me a small gift, but it was indeed weighty with significance. It was just a little bulldozer, a small caterpillar Tonka toy, but he said I would need to be like a bulldozer to straighten out the roads and pave the pathway to total joint replacement in Columbus. It truly was a metaphor of what the future held for me.

Part 2

A Compelling
Call

CHAPTER 7

Return to Columbus

Fire up the bulldozer, let's move the rock.

The transition from working in the fellowship program in Boston to opening an office in Columbus proved one of the most difficult periods of my
life. How does one start a practice, particularly a specialty surgical practice, in a metropolitan area of more than one million people? Orthopaedic
surgeons were already numerous in this city, and although most of them
were busy, they were very concerned about new competition coming into
the community. I assumed the best strategy would be to join my two resident colleagues in their practice of general orthopaedics, and then gradually build into a specialty practice. I assumed they had patients in their
practice with arthritis of the hip, and that once I began to perform total
hip replacement, the word would spread that a new treatment option
was now available for the arthritic patient.

I entered the Columbus orthopaedic community by attending the
weekly morning conferences at Ohio State University. I recall how
unfriendly the physicians were when I first entered the room. I expected
a cordial greeting such as "How are you?" or "Nice to have you back."
I was even expecting interest, such as "How was your experience in
Boston and what can you teach us about this hip replacement operation?"
But instead all they offered was a blank stare or an utterly impersonal
response. I walked to the back of the room and remained silent, wondering if this was the way it was always going to be. Was this cold reception a hint that I would be unable to fulfill my dream as a total joint
replacement surgeon?

For a few months Kelly and I lived with her parents. Our little boys were happy to be with their grandparents, and although it was pleasant for us all to be together, the imposition was evident. I began to practice general orthopaedics, which involved taking emergency room call, working late at night with trauma patients, treating and stabilizing fractures, then seeing patients during the day in the office. The office patient population came with numerous complaints: sore knees, bad backs, sore feet, stiff shoulders. When I did not see arthritis of the hip in any patient, my dream began to fade. How was I going to preserve this special knowledge and operation?

I continued to attend orthopaedic conferences and was eager to participate in the conference agenda. Finally I was asked to present Grand Rounds on the subject of total joint replacement. Grand Rounds is an important conference, attended by the entire orthopaedic community, which then was citywide. The forum opened, and I had the opportunity to describe this operation and its application. When I finished, so few questions were asked it was as if no one really cared. I began to question why this new treatment option was not being embraced. Was it my manner in the presentation? Or perhaps a fear or caution of untested technology? Their indifference continued to bother me. I believed that I did not have time to wait to share this valuable information.

Then it occurred to me that perhaps the best way to introduce the operation was through the orthopaedic residency program at Ohio State. I contacted the chief resident and began attending the arthritis clinic with him. One day a woman came to the clinic and I recognized her from my hometown. She had rheumatoid arthritis in both hips, and I had never seen arthritis this severe in my entire experience in Boston. I worked with the resident, we gained permission from the department chairman, Dr. Curtis, and we scheduled the hip replacements approximately two months apart. I was concerned about this operation, especially with the resident performing the majority of the surgery, but I believed that if I did not get started somewhere, my dream would die.

One of my greatest concerns about proceeding with this operation was the lack of appropriate surgical instruments; no one had the tools to perform a total hip replacement as I had been trained. I contacted a local instrument sales representative and selected all the instruments I needed for the surgery. I borrowed the money to pay for the instruments myself because they were extremely expensive, but I believed I was investing in the future. The load of surgical tools was enormous, three or four large leather bags. I took these instruments into the operating room and laid them out on the table, explaining to the nurses exactly how each instrument was used and when it was needed during the operation. We spent hours going over these instruments.

Interestingly enough, the nurse I had pushed out the door in the incident that resulted in my being fired during my residency took a special interest in what I was doing. She was very cordial, and she truly helped me greatly in the assimilation of this surgery at the hospital. She saw the future for this operation and laid the foundation in the nursing service for my pathway through the OR maze. In the process she and I became close friends.

At the time I opened my practice, two prosthetic designs were available. One was designed by John Charnley in England and referred to as a Charnley hip. The other was designed by Maurice Mueller and was referred to as a Charnley-Mueller hip. The Charnley-Mueller prosthesis was more popular in the United States because it was easier to insert without requiring removal of the greater trochanter, a major bone landmark at the top of the femur. I learned to do total hip replacement in Boston with the Charnley-Mueller hip, so initially it was my implant of choice. I called Dr. Turner in Boston to have him send a hip prosthesis for the operation, and I applied for a cement license from the FDA and it was granted.

Finally, the day came in late January 1971 for the first total hip replacement in Columbus, Ohio. We were scheduled to perform two total joint replacements that day at the University Hospital. They included an elderly man with a typical osteoarthritic hip, and the woman with rheumatoid arthritis. The elderly man's hip replacement would not be difficult to do, but the woman's case could be challenging. Therefore, we decided to do her surgery first. I arose very early that morning and went to the hospital with all my tools. The instruments were placed in trays in the autoclave for sterilization and then prepared in time for surgery at seven o'clock. By the time we had the patient positioned on the operating table and under anesthesia, the instruments laid out, the prosthesis selected, and the acrylic cement prepared in the appropriate apparatus, it was after nine o'clock before we began to operate. The surgical field became quite bloody. I realized that the anesthesiologist was concerned about the potential for hypotension, and he was afraid the patient's blood pressure would drop when we applied the cement into the femoral canal. So he maintained a state of higher blood pressure, which caused excessive bleeding and made it difficult for us to do the surgery. We packed the

wound to slow the blood loss and spent valuable operating time cauterizing the bleeding vessels before we could proceed with the surgery.

I started the procedure by making the incision and then gave the knife
to the resident to allow him to continue. It became obvious that he was
unable to perform the operation, even under my direction. I took the
knife back and went through the hip anatomy step-by-step as I had been
trained. I thought of nothing but each individual step that I had memorized and practiced over and over again during my fellowship and also
in my mind. The hip opened like a book, each layer was methodically
pulled back, and suddenly I was in the center of this woman's hip. We
tried to dislocate the hip, an integral step in this procedure, but it was
extremely tight because of the fibrous tissue that had developed with her
arthritis. I remembered Dr. Aufranc repeating, "Gently stretch the tissue, do not force it." I patiently stretched the tissue repeatedly, we heard
the "pop," and the hip dislocated very nicely. We removed the femoral
head, mixed the bone cement, positioned the implant, and implanted
the device in the patient's hip. We reduced the components, repaired the
muscle, and closed the wound.

The surgery was lengthy because I had to do everything in the operating room, maintain constant dialogue with the scrub nurse, and point
to each instrument that I needed during the surgery. I felt as though I
was on a football field and had to play every position. I also needed to
ensure that the bone cement was mixed correctly, including stirring and
timing the cement, and properly applying it to the surface of the bone.
A known fact about bone cement is that it has the capacity to harden in
about eight minutes. Once it is set, the cement becomes hard as rock. I
was concerned about the cement setting before the appropriate time, but
fortunately it was timed correctly, and the operation went on to the next
stage without additional complications or challenges. The surgery was
completed about one o'clock in the afternoon, and we decided to move
on to the second case.

It took another two hours to re-sterilize the instruments, clean the operating room, prepare the next patient, and set the stage for his operation.
The man's surgery proceeded slowly because I allowed the resident to do
most of the dissection. I prepared the bone surfaces and the bone cement
and inserted the implant because he had not learned these procedural
steps yet. The resident closed the wound. This operation also took
approximately four hours to complete and we finished about seven
o'clock in the evening. I had been up since four o'clock that morning

and had not stopped to eat or drink, but I really had not noticed. My body was strong and my mind was sharp; I was confident with my ability.

This was indeed a special day. I thought how extraordinary it was to bring an operation of this caliber to Columbus, Ohio, and to perform a life-changing event for two patients who could truly benefit from it. Kelly and I had anticipated this day for a long time, and she met me at our favorite restaurant to enjoy a celebration dinner. We ordered T-bone steaks with all the extras and had a big chocolate dessert. She had to drive me home afterward because I was exhausted. When I fell into bed that night I thought of the bulldozer analogy, and I knew I had finally moved the rock.

I was at the hospital early the next morning because I feared something might happen to either patient that would blight the operation. I was very attentive to their conditions. I looked at their wounds, and they were minimally swollen. The patients were bright and alert, breathing well, and moving about in bed. I commenced then to initiate the therapy programs I had been taught by Dr. Aufranc, which were foreign concepts to the physical therapist. I showed each patient how to self-exercise. I taught the therapist how to help the patients move in bed without damaging their new hip. I instructed them on how to get on and off the bedpan. I even removed the bedpan on several occasions for each patient, to make sure they understood how to maneuver correctly. The patients were kept in bed for approximately five days and then allowed to sit on the edge of the bed for two days. By the end of the week, they would begin to walk with a walker, and then advance to crutches. Patients undergoing hip replacement were in the hospital between ten and twenty days depending upon their rehabilitative course. By the time they left the hospital they were walking independently with crutches, had begun to ride a stationary bicycle, and were beginning to use their hip in a normal fashion. Actually many of the patients had to be held back from overexercising because, after being in pain for so long, they were now experiencing pain-free function and good motion from this operation. It was extremely gratifying to see the individuals who had experienced intractable pain relieved almost overnight of that arthritic condition, and to have the hip functioning to a point that they could move about independently and gain confidence in their function.

I knew a landmark event had occurred with these two surgical events, but still no additional patients appeared, no arthritic patients were referred to me, word of mouth did not appear to spread the news, and I waited and waited. I continued to practice general orthopaedics. The days and weeks went by and still no new patients appeared with hip disease. I saw myself continually as losing ground and losing the foothold on my dream. I felt as if my skills were being diluted by the general orthopaedic practice where I worked. It was paying our bills, but I was losing my spirit.

I was contacted by my mentors in Boston and invited to participate in a symposium promoting a new hip prosthesis they had designed. The designing surgeons would present the new prosthetic device to the orthopaedic community and tout its features and nuances. I was honored for the opportunity to participate in the symposium, although my assignment was rather meager. I was to be the first assistant to Dr. William Murray, an internationally renowned surgeon and professor of orthopaedic surgery from the University of California, who had been working with the Boston group to develop this new prosthesis. He would demonstrate the surgical technique under closed circuit television to a group of orthopaedic surgeons. I had not met him prior to this occasion, and I was somewhat intimidated by his strong personality.

The operation commenced. He was very verbal, talking his way through each step of the operation. When it was time to insert the stem into the canal of the femur, he placed the cement first and waited the standard four minutes for the cement to become doughy. The room was very hot, which sped the setting time. Dr. Murray was distracted by a question from the audience, and I could see the cement was very close to setting and that time was expiring to insert the prosthesis. I am not certain what came over me, but I elbowed him in the ribs and said, "Get the prosthesis in. It's setting up." He stopped, grabbed the prosthesis, and drove it in with a big hammer, and placed it just in time for the cement setting. At certain times you must move quickly to avoid disaster, and yet you must have time to think and react. Some have said that the operating room is not a place to think, but rather a place to execute, perform, and react. The dynamics are so variable, but with experience you are better able to handle the variables. After the operation was completed, Dr. Murray wanted to know who I was and immediately told me he was indebted to me for saving him from a very embarrassing situation. We became close friends. Throughout his professional lifetime he remained a father figure and a source of support to me.

Each day on my way to work I drove by a small office building. One day a vacancy sign appeared on this little office, and I thought it might be an opportunity for me to go out on my own. Despite the fact that as yet I had no arthritis patients, I thought if I did not try it on my own, my dream would die. So I took the big step. I went to the bank and arranged for a business loan and also some money to provide a livelihood. Although I was still drawing a small salary from the practice with my colleagues, I was unable to meet the economic demands of paying for the instruments I had purchased and maintaining the payments on the debts I had incurred during training. Therefore, I went to a financial adviser, and we devised a plan to borrow money to allow a frugal living. This plan included the hope that if I could perform one total joint replacement each month, I would have the same kind of lifestyle and income I had been accustomed to as a resident. Certainly this income was meager by the world's standards, but it would allow me to continue for the next six months. So I went to my colleagues and told them I was going out on my own. I appreciated the opportunity they had given me to work with them, but my heart and soul was in practicing total joint replacement, and if I did not try, I would never know its potential.

So I opened my own office. The interior was very small. There was one exam room, one room for an X-ray machine, a little space for an office, a secretary's desk, and a reception area. I waited as patiently as I could for patients to come, anticipating that someone would start referring patients to me or that the patients themselves might learn about this technology through the media and appear on my office doorstep.

Kelly worked in the office until I was able to hire a secretary, who then called various doctors' offices on the phone with information about total hip replacement technology and the fact that it was now available in the Columbus area. She avoided the orthopaedic surgical community, focusing instead on the family practice and general practitioner section of the city where this new technology was beginning to come into awareness. After a few short weeks, she started to schedule patients. I remember how elated I was when she called me, no matter where I was, to tell me a new patient had scheduled an examination.

Another effective strategy was to work in cooperation with other orthopaedic surgeons in the area who had patients that needed hip surgery. These surgeons were reluctant to refer patients out of their practices, so I went to the doctor and proposed that both of us perform the surgery. They accepted my help with the surgery so that they could offer the new technology to their patients. The very act of doing the surgery and the fact that it was still so unusual piqued a tremendous amount of curiosity and discussion among the medical personnel in the area.

It became common knowledge that I was responsible for bringing this technology to the community and that I was performing the operation with a system of organization and expertise heretofore unknown in other orthopaedic surgical venues. I visited the patients both before and after the operation but never told them I was the primary person in the surgical scenario. But really, I did everything: I performed the surgery, wrote the orders, prescribed the physical therapy, and educated the OR and floor staff as well as the physical therapists. I spent hours at the hospital after surgery with both the staff and the patients, helping them learn the therapeutic systems to ensure success. The staff were eager students, just like the residents, wanting to learn about this new technology. I found teaching them to be one of the most rewarding experiences of this time. Their receptivity, like that of the residents, was the only positive reinforcement I received, and I craved this sense of fulfillment. They expressed surprise that a doctor would spend so much time at the hospital with them and with the patients.

My biggest worry was the potential for a serious surgical or postoperative complication, which would blight this revolutionary procedure. I had some close calls. One woman had intense bleeding during the surgery; the blood seemed to be coming from behind the pelvis and I was terribly afraid that I had run the power reamer into the pelvic vessels. I lifted the muscle from the beam of the pelvis and proceeded inside the abdominal wall where I was able to identify the blood vessel and correct the problem. I had never explored that part of the anatomy, and afterward I realized the risk involved as well as the intensity of my fear. However, I met with success and the patient went on to do very well. Another woman had the unusual finding of a venous plexus (a series of blood vessels) over her hip that I was completely unaware of before surgery. As I exposed this region of the hip, blood filled the wound, gushing everywhere. Initially, I did not know what to do. Then I remembered an incident during my vascular surgery rotation: when the bleeding was heavy, the surgeon would take a surgical sponge or two and press very hard on the vessels. This stopped the bleeding momentarily, allowing the surgeon time to identify the source and stitch the openings in the veins. I followed this technique and was amazed at how effective it was in this woman. These incidents illustrate the fact that, no matter how thorough your training, you can never anticipate everything that might happen in a case. The learning curve continues constant throughout your entire career.

My Boston connection endured, as I was called on numerous occasions to promote the new prosthesis being developed by the Boston surgeons. It was the first of a series of prostheses to come forth as the orthopaedic manufacturing industry entered a phase of rapid growth. The development of these prostheses was based on speculative knowledge as to what might work better, but the basic implant design remained unchanged. I promoted the new prosthesis in the Midwest by encouraging encounters with various orthopaedic surgeons in Ohio. This opportunity offered the setting to make the acquaintance of surgeons who either were already performing joint replacement or were interested in learning the techniques. I met surgeons from Cincinnati, Dayton, and Cleveland.

I remember one time when I went to meet with the orthopaedic surgeons at the University of Cincinnati. A biomedical engineering student completing work toward his doctorate in bioengineering, Dane Miller, had designed a hip simulator to test hip prostheses, which applied forces across a given geometry of the implant. This simulator would allow the interpretation of these forces to determine which prosthetic design was most appropriate, and moreover, how it was tolerating such stresses as wear, bend, and load. Miller was a bright, soft-spoken young man, very enthusiastic about his research. We immediately struck up a friendship. After he graduated from the University of Cincinnati and received his doctorate in bioengineering, he was hired by one of the top orthopaedic companies to work in their engineering department. Some years later he formed his own company, Biomet, which became a leader in orthopaedic manufacturing.

These promotional efforts of mine provoked controversy within the orthopaedic community, as I did also when I contacted the county medical societies around the state of Ohio and offered to come to their local meetings to lecture about total joint replacement. By today's standards this form of information sharing would be considered relatively innocuous, but in those days such presentations were considered a form of advertising and promotion. The county medical society presentations provided a great number of patients who were good candidates for total hip replacement.

Meanwhile, back in the operating room, I had made a commitment to surgical excellence. I memorized the steps of the operation so that each move was predetermined. If I did encounter an unexpected situation, I modified the process but never abandoned the scheduled steps; it worked amazingly well. One of the greatest challenges was to work with a surgical nurse who was unfamiliar with total hip replacement and the instruments required. Often I was forced to play two roles: the first to operate and the second to manage the scrub nurse. The surgical assistant across the table from me also had to be coordinated, but this was relatively easy because his or her role was more passive. Initially the first assistant was another nurse, a resident, or another physician.

Ensuring the precision of the surgical routine and the exact postoperative agenda was very important to me. As I gained experience, the time of the actual operation lessened to approximately two hours. More time was wasted trying to initiate the surgical procedure into the existing OR system. Delays included anesthesia, nurse setups, cleaning and preparing the room for the next case, and schedule delays from other cases. These are encumbrances encountered by a surgeon in the operating room of any hospital; it can be very difficult to be efficient. In between operations I spent a lot of time on the hospital ward with the patients during their recovery phase. I personally went through the physical therapy program with each patient. I made sure that the program was well supervised and that each therapist was fully cognizant of my system. One technique I learned from Dr. Aufranc was especially effective. He told me that if you teach a patient before the operation how to move in bed and out of bed, it would keep their pain medications to a minimum and increase their postoperative comfort.

My time at the University Hospital lessened as I went to work with other doctors in the community. I began doing surgery at two major private hospitals, which meant I had patients to see at all three hospitals. I spent considerable time in the car, driving to do my rounds, so I would not start my surgery schedule in one hospital until I had made the rounds at the other hospitals first. I soon tired of coordinating a dysfunctional schedule. I began to start rounds at the first hospital about half past four or five in the morning. These were odd hours to be in the hospital, but I found it effective. Most patients were awake because they were in some degree of discomfort or they were in a stage of light sleep because the hospital was very noisy. The patients did not mind that I came in so early, and it allowed me to spend quality time with each patient. Even those patients who had first appeared reserved and private grew to be quite friendly. Each patient and I would become a team, working closely with the medical staff that was serving his or her hospital needs.

I was fortunate in those early days that I did not experience any major complications, which could have shrouded the procedure in uncertainty.

For the sake of prevention, all my patients were on prophylactic antibiotics so the wound infection issue was minimal. However, one man developed a pneumococcal infection in the hip some four to six weeks after his total hip replacement. How could this particular bug, which primarily occupies the respiratory tract and the lungs, be found in his hip? I learned that he had suffered an episode of pneumonia after his total hip replacement, so I concluded that the infection must have spread from his lung to the hip. This phenomenon had not been discussed previously in the medical literature, so I quickly wrote the case report and submitted it to the *Journal of Bone and Joint Surgery*. The article was accepted, and now I had a piece published in a major medical journal. I saw the opportunity to write about my patients and my experience because I was ahead of the pack, not only in Columbus, but also around the country. Some surgeons studied, worked, and prepared themselves for years to negotiate the medical literature process before their work was accepted and placed in the archives. I was not even board certified and I had a paper accepted. I was so encouraged by this effort that I decided to publish as much about total hip replacement as I possibly could, and I found this to be a good discipline because the critical nature of the editorial reviews sharpened my capacity to write medical literature.

I had opportunity to report another complication of hip replacement surgery. During one case a resident pushed too hard on the acetabular reamer, which chewed through the bone of the socket, and it sank into the pelvis and cut the main blood vessel. A vascular surgeon in the next room came rushing in, turned the patient onto his back, opened his belly, stopped the bleeding, and saved the patient's life. That incident was well contained within the dynamics of its circumstances. I wrote a case report describing the caveat and submitted it to a journal. It was published as a warning to avoid the potential complications of over-reaming during bone preparation. This unfortunate occurrence served as a hallmark case in the literature, which helped prevent many future incidents.

This episode illustrates the challenges of surgical resident education. On one hand an inexperienced resident is in the process of developing surgical skills, which means he or she must operate. On the other hand, the patient has contracted with the primary surgeon and, in good faith, deserves a certain level of expertise. This creates a conflict. In the OSU teaching hospitals where I was introducing this operation, I was committed to the patient's well-being, but I felt the pressure of letting the surgeon-in-training develop his surgical skills. I have always believed it is important to support the educational system to allow the surgeon-trainees to develop their skills. These young doctors learned a great deal under my supervision, and for the most part they did very well.

During this time the family moved to a small farm outside the metropolitan area of Columbus. I would come home late in the evenings, play with my boys until their bedtime, and then have a late supper with Kelly. This arrangement was not satisfactory, because I had made a commitment long before we had children that I would spend meaningful time with them during their young years. I knew from personal experience that once they were teenagers and began high school they would be preoccupied. So I changed my schedule: I continued the early morning rounds, performed surgery in the morning, saw patients at the office in the afternoon, finished about four o'clock in the afternoon, and went home to spend time with my boys. The distance added to my drive time, but I enjoyed the glimpses of country life sandwiched between the long arduous hours in my practice.

CHAPTER 8

A Speciality Practice
in Joint Replacement

If it's going to be, it's up to me.

I had Charnley's hip center model in my mind from the first day I opened my solo practice. I had already realized that I must be the main player in all these systems at the time, directing the clinic, performing the surgery, managing the surgical staff, and directing the physical therapy and rehabilitation regimen. I was an active participant in the therapy instruction, which developed the strong doctor-patient relationship I thought important for my position. Until my clinic and operating schedules filled, I was able to spend time talking with my patients, instructing the hospital staff, and personally directing the patients' physical therapy. I knew it was essential that the patient, as well as the nursing staff observing, understood the precautions necessary to avoid dislocation and any other inappropriate activities that might endanger the patient's hip implant.

Because this agenda kept me on the hospital floor for periods of time, I became well acquainted with the nursing staff. I noticed that one young man was particularly interested in my patients because he would follow me into the patients' rooms and ask appropriate questions. I learned he was interested in becoming a physician, perhaps even a surgeon. I was particularly impressed with his genuineness. He became competent at assisting me with the patients' therapy and knowledgeable of the proper way to use a walker and initiate the gait-training program.

One morning we went to assist an older man in his first attempt to sit on the edge of the bed and stand. The patient was an unusual individual; he was an immigrant who spoke with broken English, and his son had played football with my brother at Miami University. At times he

appeared quite disturbed by the whole hospital experience. He had difficulty understanding my instructions, but I was as kind, gentle, and
patient as I could be in explaining to him that together we were going to
get him out of bed so that he could stand on his new hip for the first
time. He was apprehensive as we started to get him off the bed and into
a standing position, so we went very slowly, continuing to encourage him.
Just as the patient placed his hands on the walker, he fell backward, desperately waving his hands and grasping for anything to slow the impact
of the fall. He was a big strong man with large hands. His hands struck
the chest of the male attendant and slid down his chest to his groin. The
man's grasp was so tight he pulled the male attendant to the floor along
with him. As they both lay prostrate on the floor howling in pain, I saw
blood gushing from the male attendant's groin area.

The commotion caught the attention of several passing nurses and they
rushed into the room to attend the patient. Meanwhile, I was focused on
the male attendant because his bleeding was profuse. I applied pressure to
slow the blood flow and, upon investigating the wound, saw that the scro-
tum was torn almost completely from his body. I quickly got him on a cart
and headed to the operating room where a urologist repaired the damaged
genitals. The recovery was difficult and the poor man became infertile. He
lost the desire to become a physician and, after much counseling, became
a businessman. The last time I saw him he was doing reasonably well.
Meanwhile the patient never did gain mobility despite numerous attempts
to educate him on the proper use of the walker. He later developed dementia, became bedfast, and expired in a nursing home. As I think back on the
occasion, I am reminded again of how complicated life can get. Who could
imagine such a horrible thing happening to this fine young man? Sometimes
life is tragically unfair. I found it difficult to maintain an upbeat attitude
for days after that experience. But then again, what other alternative was
there for me but to go on and perform another hip replacement and continue to assist the patient at the bedside?

During this early phase of my practice, I had frequent encounters with
the orthopaedic residents at Ohio State University. One resident, David
Halley, seemed particularly drawn to me. He was a bright and energetic
young man who was finishing his orthopaedic residency and considering
his future. One day he told me he wanted to take a fellowship as I did and
asked my recommendation. I suggested he consider the Harvard fellowship, but more important, I encouraged him to try to secure a registrar position with Charnley in England. In my opinion Charnley's practice was on

the cutting edge in joint replacement surgery at that time. Halley heeded the advice, went through the application process, and was selected for a position as a registrar at Charnley's hip center in Wrightington, England.

So the Halleys went to England and Kelly and I went to visit them while they were there. I was very impressed with what I observed on my second visit to Charnley's hip center, including the close relationship that had developed between Halley and Charnley. They were good friends, and Halley worked hard to distinguish himself not only in patient care and surgical education but also in the writing of an important scientific manuscript, which even today is a classic.

When Halley returned to Columbus, we joined forces for a while, but we did not have a large enough practice to support both of us financially. Halley's time and effort in England added greatly to the dissemination of joint replacement technology in Columbus.

I realized that the arthritic condition also was common in the knee and that the demand for total knee replacement would follow on the wings of total hip replacement. In order to meet the patients' needs I would have to know how to perform both procedures. At that time total knee replacement was in its infancy, and most of the refinement of this procedure and technology was occurring in the United States. A series of different knee designs had been developed, but they were all elementary. So I went on to the Mayo Clinic in Rochester, Minnesota, and watched the surgeons perform total knee replacement with the polycentric design. I then performed the first total knee replacement in Columbus in the summer of 1971 using the polycentric knee system. This patient had a good result.

A young man came to me with a painful knee just as I was beginning to perform knee replacement. He was an attorney, had been diagnosed with rheumatoid arthritis, and was interested in knee replacement to alleviate his pain. Upon surgical entry to the knee joint, I was surprised to find that the patient's articular cartilage was in good condition, but the synovium was thickened. So, I performed a synovectomy instead of the planned total knee replacement. After surgery I reviewed my findings with him and thought he would be as delighted as I was that we had avoided a major operation. He was grim when I told him I had not performed a total knee replacement even though it was in my best judgment not to perform it. I explained that he should not have this operation prematurely because the prosthesis had a finite durability. Less than six weeks later, I received a notice that this man was suing me. He claimed that the procedure performed on the knee was done without informed consent. This was the first lawsuit of my career, but others would follow. I cannot express the disappointment, the chagrin, the anguish, and the deep depression that came over me when this patient sued me. The lawsuit stemmed from a miscommunication, a misunderstanding, despite my best efforts to do the right thing.

My malpractice insurance company provided an outstanding defense lawyer who was much my senior. He warned me that my occupation was at considerable risk for lawsuits and encouraged me to do all I could to practice informed consent and to stay realistic. Most important, he advised me that if I should encounter difficulty, I should never abandon my patients or lay blame on them. I have always remembered his advice, though sometimes I found it hard to comply with as I continued to practice surgery for thirty years.

So because the knee technology at this point was still developing, I focused my practice again on the comfort and security of the hip replacement procedure. I kept my eye on the progress of knee replacement, however. I knew that eventually the biomechanical engineers would develop a successful device.

My practice was growing; I was doing four or five hip replacements a week, which was remarkable considering the scarcity of patients. Actually, many people suffered from arthritis of the hip, but they were hesitant to try the new operation. Some patients might have been held in the offices of practitioners who yet were skeptical about its effectiveness. However, my four or five cases a week afforded plenty of time for me to write my presentations for the orthopaedic courses and to teach the residents some new aspects of joint replacement technology.

One day Dane Miller, the biomedical engineer I had met at the University of Cincinnati, walked into my office with an unusual request. After a short stint in the corporate orthopaedic world, Miller had begun the development of his independent company, Biomet. He pulled a hip prosthesis out of his pocket, the first such implant to be produced at Biomet, and he asked if I would place it into his grandmother's arthritic hip. I was taken aback by the great confidence he had in what he was creating. Here was a budding entrepreneur with enough assurance in his work that he was willing to have it implanted in a member of his immediate family. I agreed to do the surgery, and his grandmother subsequently did very well. A few years later Miller and I would reconnect again when Biomet helped to develop the Mallory-Head hip system (see Figure 5).

Figure 5. The Mallory-Head hip system, designed by Tom Mallory and William Head in the 1980s.

As my operating-room schedule became busier, it was difficult to transport the instruments to multiple hospitals and work with a different scrub nurse at each location. I began to seek a scrub nurse who was capable of directing the operating room, maintaining, cleaning, and storing the instruments as well as transporting them from hospital to hospital. I chose a nurse who had a work ethic similar to my own. I invested hours of my time teaching her the details of the operation and the instrumentation. Soon she could organize my operations and methodically assist with their execution to the point that we could operate without even speaking to one another. I realized that developing a good team was a key element in being an excellent surgeon, that each facet of the operation needed to be synchronized. Enlisting her help meant that we took approximately one hour off the operating room time, which shortened the surgical procedure, minimized blood loss, and produced consistent efficiency.

The next team to build was in the postoperative phase of the patient's hospital stay, the physical therapy aspect, to optimize rehabilitation. I found a nurse who was very interested in the joint replacement patients, and I taught her all I knew about the physical therapy regimen. While I was in surgery, she was teaching the therapy to the patients. So thanks to the dedicated efforts of these nurses and their significant roles in the process, I was able to increase my workload capacity.

I worked harder and faster, and as a result my organization grew immensely as I became more experienced and more efficient. However, the complexity of the surgery increased with the greater variety of patients coming to me for surgery, and I discovered more problems. I recall one case that I performed with my nurse; she was the lone surgical assistant on that day. The patient was a woman who was quite heavy, and it was difficult to properly position the leg to gain adequate visibility into the hip joint. I dissected through the layers into the hip area and dislocated it as was the standard procedure, then I placed the leg over the side of the operating table and left it unsupported. I could see into the hip joint this way, and we completed the surgery without difficulty. I realized my mistake when the patient awoke with sciatic nerve palsy (nerve dysfunction) because of the stretching of the nerve that occurred while her leg hung off the operating table. She was screaming with pain in the recovery room, and then when she realized she could not move her foot, she was inconsolable. I tried to comfort her, but her pain was excruciating. She had sported a rather sour personality prior to surgery, and this certainly did not add to her persona. She was furious with me and would not allow me into her room. It is surprising that she never sued me, but she fired me instead. I was unable to pursue the complication or to treat her. As far as I know the nerve never recovered, and she was permanently disabled. Needless to say, this incident left a lasting impression on me. I never again left the leg unsupported during the operation.

On one of the early knee replacements I performed, I actually operated on the wrong leg! The patient had bilateral knee osteoarthritis, so I suppose in the long run it did not matter, and I was fortunate that neither the patient nor I suffered any repercussions. It was an oversight in the operating room, I missed it, and it served to warn me of the danger of this happening on a patient who did not need bilateral knee replacement. I then began to have the patient mark his or her own extremity so that the nurse could witness it before I started the operation. It should be an impossible occurrence, but it happens even in the best of operating rooms. I found it good practice to address those issues of a potentially dangerous nature and deal with them in a scheduled format.

The success of an operation results from the success of a series of steps. What is perceived to be the most important part of the operation includes insertion of the implant, and the balance and appropriate fixation of the components in the right space and of the right size. Another important aspect is the way in which the hip is surgically opened and dissected, with minimal blood loss and trauma to the tissue. The last aspect is the method of wound closure. I stressed optimum wound closure above other aspects because it usually was not emphasized during training and could flaw the whole procedure.

Wound infection was one of the most dreaded complications. Even with the use of prophylactic (preventative) antibiotics and a clean air environment in the operating room, a patient occasionally would develop an infection despite all these measures. When an infection occurred, patients required immediate and aggressive treatment. Often my first thought was that I had not kept the environment clean enough, or that I had inadvertently contaminated the wound during the case. Guilt overrides good judgment at times, so I found it was important to approach an infection objectively, to suppress my feelings of guilt and simply give the patient good care. To overcome this hurdle, I would not tolerate anything but the cleanest of wounds. In fact, I taught my residents that the wound-healing process was most important, and that unless you had a good wound you did not have a good operation. When I recognized a wound issue, I would limit the patient's activity and aggressively treat and drain it. If the wound still did not heal, I would open it again, clean it, and re-suture it. There was a group of patients, however, that sustained wound infections no matter what I did. I could have the best operation, and the cleanest environment, I could use prophylactic antibiotics, and still the patient became infected. A 100 percent infection-free practice does not exist. Although it was an infrequent complication, it was a serious issue.

In addition, expediting the closure was important because once the volume of surgery increased, the time spent closing the wound was important. My next question was, Could someone else close the wound as well as I, and in a short period of time? Hiring such a person would free me from that part of the operation and allow me time to dictate the operative notes, interface with a previous patient, or prepare for the next operation. I soon would discover the answer.

These incidents of infection, sciatic palsy, prosthetic dislocation, and litigious encounters with patients all were part of the education process that I did not acquire in residency. Only the years of practice and the experience of numbers of patients could teach these lessons. A formal medical school education is not all-inclusive but simply provides the tools by which a surgeon can expand his or her information base.

My presence in Columbus continued to be controversial within the local orthopaedic community. I was walking on turf they claimed as their own. Even when a local surgeon would allow me to assist with the surgery, it was a cold and indifferent atmosphere. I recalled how cordial my interactions had been with them when I was a resident, but now that I was a finished practitioner working in the community, the sense of compatibility and camaraderie we had shared had dissipated. But I did respect the rapport I was gaining with the young residents; they eagerly embraced what I was doing and recognized that I was participating in a new generation. They started to call me "Chief." When I look back on those years, I realize I was extremely aggressive, but I was passionate about a marvelous new technology.

CHAPTER 9

The Hip Center
at St. Ann's Hospital

Focus is the secret; one idea, one goal, one dream.

By 1974 my practice, my patient base, and my surgery schedule were growing at such a rapid rate that I could not contain it within a single hospital setting. The hospital systems in Columbus all were inundated with a great plethora of operative procedures performed by a number of surgeons. Here I was, a young doctor with a single surgical procedure that required special time and services to accomplish, and my caseload was not at all attractive to the hospital administrators. However, I knew I could fill a hospital floor and keep a couple of operating rooms busy if I just had an opportunity to create a "mini hip center" concept. One day I came to my office and found a notice on my desk that St. Ann's Hospital was opening its doors to a medical and surgical practice. St. Ann's Hospital was located in the inner city section of Columbus in a very unattractive setting. The buildings were old, the streets were dirty, the area was unsafe with rampant crime, and the days were darkened by the smog that hung over the region.

Nevertheless, I got in my car and drove over to explore this blighted area. St. Ann's Hospital had been built in the early 1900s, and the additions to the original brick building were not architecturally pleasing. The parking lot was gravel. I walked through an archway leading to the hospital entrance and stepped into an atmosphere made dismal by poor lighting, dark floors, stark decor, and a feeling of hopelessness. I found the elevator and rode up a couple of floors to the administrative area. The nursing and administrative dimensions were run by a Catholic order, and I met with the sister administrator to explain my idea of a mini hip

85

center. She was enthusiastic about the proposal because she had heard about joint replacement technology, and she did not think it unreasonable to dedicate an entire floor of the hospital to develop a center such as I described. Although the hospital had been known for its excellent obstetrics and gynecology service, its patrons had been lost during the suburban sprawl in the early 1970s, leaving forty-six beds in the hospital empty. I saw this as an ideal situation where there was no competition. She offered that the hospital would be willing to invest a certain amount of money for improvements. They were also willing to build a special laminar airflow operating room that was beneficial for maintaining a sterile environment.

I was elated with the prospect because this was exactly what I had been searching for. Here was the place where I could develop a hip center and organize it according to the successful model I had seen during my travels abroad and around the country. I left the hospital that day with a great thankfulness in my heart that they had accepted my proposal. But other questions still remained. Could a hip center work in a ghetto area? Was there a danger of being robbed or molested in pursuit of a good operation? Even after such consideration I decided to go for it. After all, the hospital where I had trained in Boston was in a similar neighborhood.

The five existing operating rooms were dismal and small, and the patient rooms were dark. It took approximately six months to refurbish the patient rooms and almost a year to completely reconstruct the operating room. I did not wait for the construction to be finished but, rather, began operating immediately. Because I was involved with the reconstruction from the very beginning, I approved everything from the size of the operating room to the decor of the patient rooms. I remember the coat of light blue paint on the walls that enlivened the patient rooms, and the sunlight that infused warmth and hope when I insisted that all the blinds be opened in the patient rooms during the day. I specified the kinds of nurses to employ and the clinical pathways to be instituted. Two small operating rooms would be combined into one large operating room dedicated to my patients. Once this was completed, it was a dream to work in, not only because it incorporated this new laminar airflow technology to ensure a sterile field but also because we had plenty of space to work. I was fortunate because the anesthesia group supporting St. Ann's Hospital was well grounded and well trained.

It seemed too good to be true, but the lingering question remained to be answered: Would the people come if we practiced exclusively at this hospital in a ghetto? I had many friends, colleagues, and business people who told me it never would work, that patients would not come into that kind of environment just to have me operate on them. When I left an elegant private hospital in Columbus on a beautiful expanse of land, the chief of staff told me I was crazy to resign from *the* place to practice and risk my well-being and that of my patients at St. Ann's. But in the end the hospital and I disproved the naysayers. The patients did come, and within two and a half years we filled that whole floor. The patients were of all kinds and from everywhere, and their experiences were positive. The surgery went well, the nursing care was excellent, and the food was exceptional. In the five years we operated at St. Ann's, not one incident of crime occurred that I am aware of, not to me, my staff, or my patients.

I began to work at St. Ann's Hospital with a small number of patients while the construction was in process (see Figure 6). St. Ann's Hospital was very clean, with cooperative effort from the administration to initiate this new practice into their hospital. The hip center concept blossomed, and the nurses were good or better than any I had encountered in the other city hospitals. The personnel were interesting and qualified. There were nurses with graduate degrees, and medical professionals called physician assistants. A physician assistant (PA) is a specially trained practitioner with an undergraduate degree who also has spent additional time training in the operating room. St. Ann's Hospital had two PAs that assisted in the operating room.

A PA by the name of Doug Brewer was assigned to my room (see Figure 7). Doug had trained as a surgical assistant in the Marine Corps and then in college enrolled in a physician assistant program in Cleveland, Ohio, focusing primarily on surgical assisting. He was very pleasant to be around and showed a good knowledge of his assigned surgical tasks. Doug, my scrub nurse, and I spent hours rehearsing the steps of the operation, and we became a fantastic team. When I started to operate with Doug, I was amazed at how quick his hands were and how adeptly he perceived what I needed; he was focused and committed to his job as a first assistant. He never tried to do the operation, as so often was the case with the surgical residents who assisted me. He was committed to facilitating the operation in any way he could. As I began to work with him, I realized that he changed the whole nature of my surgery. He was organized and we seemed to have a silent language together. We never talked about the next move, but he knew exactly where I was going and what I was doing. He continually made it easier for me to operate the difficult

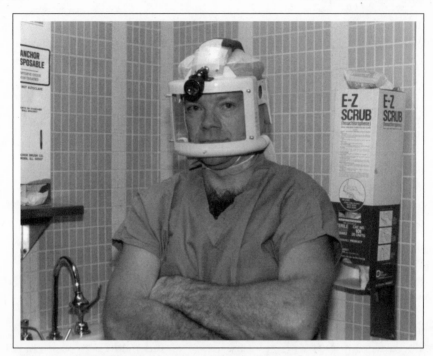

Figure 6. Tom Mallory in the OR at St. Ann's Hospital.

cases that were sent to me. We literally carved hours off the surgery to a point that we could do a hip replacement operation in less than one hour. The surgery was good, quick, delicate, focused, and organized.

My approach to the operation was somewhat similar to that of Charnley's center in England. My agenda included the use of a private scrub nurse and a skilled first assistant in surgery, with these activities located in one hospital (see Figure 8). We all could see something special evolving with this effort. We were developing a consistent format that had the capacity to handle the variants as they occurred without changing the systematic approach.

I remember one night, I was called back to the hospital because of a bleeding problem on a frail, elderly woman whose hip I had replaced that day. She was bleeding from her hip wound, and I knew I needed to take her back to the OR to investigate the bleeding. I called Doug and my private scrub nurse to help me with the case. The anesthesiologist on call was unable to intubate the patient and had sedated her lightly when he said we could begin the case. I was eager to proceed as her bleeding

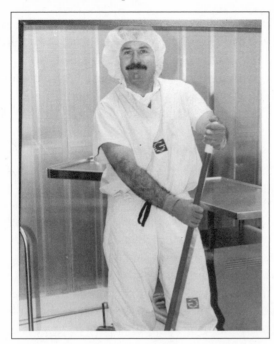

*Figure 7.
Doug Brewer, PA,
in the OR.*

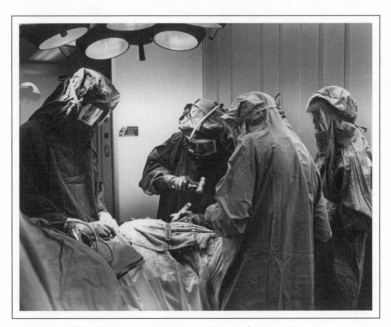

Figure 8. The OR team at St. Ann's Hospital.

was severe and I was worried she would go into cardiac arrest. As I made the skin incision and began dissecting through the tissue, she raised her head and made a loud sighing noise. I felt certain she had arrested, and I yelled at Doug, "She's dying!" I broke scrub, turned the patient onto her back, and administered a strong precordial thump to the center of her chest. As I stepped back from the table, she held her chest, sat up on the operating table, and screamed, "Oh my God, why did you have to hit me so hard in the chest?" As the anesthesiologist was scrambling to put her back to sleep, Doug and my scrub nurse were laughing hysterically at the patient's response to my presumed resuscitation!

One busy Friday we had completed three cases by noon. The last case was an elderly woman whose blood pressure had dropped drastically despite minimal blood loss during the procedure. She was stable when I saw her during rounds, but a floor nurse called that evening and said my patient was beginning to have problems with her breathing. Later in the evening a nurse called me again to report that she was stable. I arose early the next morning, a Saturday, and went to the hospital to round. I found my patient in a coma, barely living on a support system of oxygen and fluids. I immediately transferred her to the intensive care unit of a nearby hospital, more equipped for crisis care than St. Ann's. The woman eventually died, unable to recover from this episode, and we really never learned the cause of her demise. Her son, an articulate and intense lawyer from Washington, D.C., was understandably upset with the outcome of his mother's operation and the care she had received after her hip replacement. He was most upset that St. Ann's had no critical support system, intensive care unit, or crisis medicine center in this hospital. I was certain he would slap me with a big lawsuit, but he did not. He simply told me I was crazy to operate on people his mother's age in a hospital that did not have an intensive care unit. How right he was. What was I thinking?

How could I continue to operate on patients of this age group in a hospital without a support system for crisis care? I thought it would be difficult to find a group of internists willing to come to service St. Ann's Hospital, just to oversee my patients. Fortunately I had a good friend, a cardiologist, who was part of a growing group of practitioners who wanted more work. They decided as a group that they would cover my patients at St. Ann's, and they performed in-house preliminary physical examinations, prepared the patients for surgery, or cancelled the procedure if they found significant medical risk. They followed the patients closely during their hospital course. This changed the whole medical environment during the patient's stay because the internists were excellent doctors and knew exactly what to do if a crisis occurred. My patients recovered very quickly because of the internists' expert care.

All the necessary pieces were starting to fit together—the hospital, the medical staff, and the support. I still lacked an important component for this hip center, which was a physical therapy department. I still wanted very much to help with the therapy myself, but I knew that, realistically, there was a limit to what I could do. I discovered a therapist at St. Ann's with a gentle manner about her that the patients loved. She encouraged rather than forced the patients to do the exercises, and they gained confidence in their ability to mobilize with their hip implant. She built a staff of therapists around her that was very effective.

As I walked through this little hospital, I observed that few other surgeons were operating except me. The hospital was busy with my patients and the surrounding support systems of nursing, anesthesia, crisis care, and therapy. I felt blessed with a world of focus on this operation. Few surgeons if any in the United States ever had the opportunity or capacity to do something of this magnitude. The elements all were there in St. Ann's Hospital. The success of the operations and systems at St. Ann's accelerated my surgical practice of orthopaedics to a new level. The practice boomed. I was doing more joint replacements singularly than anyone in the country, in a few very short years, because of the team I was fortunate enough to assemble around me.

It became necessary to find a more convenient office location to complement the professional image and character that were emerging in my practice. As I pondered the office situation, the well-respected retired orthopaedic surgeon Henry Lacy died, and his widow listed his office building for sale. It was a stone's throw from St. Ann's Hospital and was just the type of office building I was looking to buy. It was listed for sale at a huge price, but my practice was thriving, so I bought the building and Kelly decorated it most beautifully. The patients enjoyed the old house and admired the antiques; going to the doctor became an outing in itself.

Everything was going well: the practice was growing; I had a good hospital relationship at St. Ann's; I was building a focused staff in my office, the operating room, and the hospital floor; the patients were receiving good care, and they just kept coming. It seemed as if I was in a world by myself, and none of my Columbus colleagues paid much more attention to me. Even with all the success I was enjoying in my practice, the local orthopaedic community still did not acknowledge my contributions or the significance of what I was doing. I remained on the periphery of the community, and although I continued to try to interface on various occasions, I felt a cold and isolating sense of rejection. I was sure some would have liked to see me fail, but my confidence was strong and I knew my patient care was the best. The surgery was rapid and effective, and the numbers of satisfied patients going out into the community testified to my integrity. I think the greatest element of controversy was that some thought I was practicing in an unorthodox fashion. What they did not realize, and neither did I, was that orthopaedic surgery itself was undergoing a change. Subspecialization within orthopaedic surgery had come of age.

Total joint replacement was destined to revolutionize the way patient care was being delivered. I felt that my good fortune was not only to perform the surgery but also to describe the systems, protocols, and pathways. Orthopaedic surgeons from all over the world began to come to Columbus to visit the hip center at St. Ann's Hospital. They came to see all the systems at work, and then they returned home and began to incorporate similar programs and operations in their hospitals and centers. My dream had come true. Little did I realize that my experience in the St. Ann's hip center would take me into the future in a way not even I could imagine.

The revenues generated from my practice helped to reverse the indebtedness of St. Ann's Hospital. The administration decided in 1980 to move the hospital to suburban Columbus. I chose to remain in my office, which was in the downtown Columbus area, but we moved the surgical base from St. Ann's to a nearby hospital that granted fifty hospital beds for my patients, four operating rooms, and a team of nurses and support doctors. We increased the staff but retained our core people who had originally started with me. New employees came and went, but Doug Brewer was always there.

Doug worked with me for twenty-five years. Throughout the span of our working relationship, he was never late for work, and he continuously critiqued and helped improve the program. Doug was my right-hand man. He met me early in the morning to do rounds, then he was by my side in the operating room and on the hospital floor, and eventually he worked with me seeing patients in the clinic. It is hard for me to imagine how anyone could work for someone that long and still maintain a positive, constructive working and personal relationship. Doug was my confidant and friend. We ran together after work, rode horses together, talked for hours, and visited many orthopaedic centers around the nation. When I think about the gift of another person to my career, it goes without saying that Doug Brewer sacrificed everything to facilitate my success. He was my alternative in the operating room, he taught residents how to operate, and many times he kept me out of trouble. I have been told numerous times by visiting orthopaedic surgeons that together Doug and I were unmatched when it came to speed, efficiency, skill, and capacity. When Doug accompanied me to assist at a surgical demonstration in Los Angeles, an observing surgeon asked, "Where can I find a Doug for me?" And my reply was very simple: "You will not. He does not exist."

I had implemented a practice of consistency, authenticity, and validity in the development of a multidimensional practice. Three essential elements were established in the hip center: excellent patient-care, clinical research, and a system of education for orthopaedic students, residents, and practitioners. The clinical research was an ongoing phenomenon, and I already had initiated a computerized patient database. Our electronic data recording and retrieval mechanisms were crude by today's standards, but nevertheless they were established. We maintained access to large files of patient clinical histories with various diagnoses, treatments, prosthetic combinations, and technologies. The database supported the publication of two or three papers per year in the orthopaedic literature. I hired research personnel to analyze the data and prepare the papers for publication. The presentation and publication materials were abundant because our database was sufficiently large to address questions being asked by the orthopaedic manufacturers and the orthopaedic community at large. For example, our database was extensive enough to describe the durability of the prosthesis and the best surgical techniques.

The education of orthopaedic practitioners was expanding. Although I had the opportunity to lecture nationwide at various conferences, I still did not have the opportunity to share my knowledge in an everyday setting. I decided to sponsor a fellowship program, with the hope that one day it would gain recognition and prestige. The purpose of the fellowship was to offer a beneficial term of apprenticeship in order for a young surgeon to gain valuable total joint experience. By working one-on-one with me, the fellow could participate at an intimate level that heretofore was unavailable. For example, a fellow would do some parts of the surgery, act as a surrogate in the clinic seeing patients, read and discuss the current orthopaedic literature, attend various medical education seminars, and occasionally present information as a faculty participant. The fellowship lasted between three and twelve months, but the more time spent on it the better. Once the fellow had experienced the training program, he could incorporate the area of expertise into a specialty practice similar to mine.

My first fellow came in 1977. I placed a notice for the fellowship in a widely circulated orthopaedic journal, and the first year five or six orthopaedic surgeons applied. I was delighted that they were willing to come to Columbus and study under my tutelage. Subsequently a number of the fellows who participated over the course of the years went on to focus their practices in joint replacement surgery. Some actually have become world renowned and have developed prosthetic systems, lectured internationally, and gained expertise in the field of reconstructive hip and knee surgery.

The fellowship program was one of the most rewarding and beneficial activities I have ever undertaken. I enjoyed the interaction with the fellows as their minds were young, unbiased, accepting and nonjudgmental, receptive and inquisitive, and very encouraged by the opportunity to develop skill in a growing specialty with the large momentum I had built in my practice. The fellows were with me from twelve to fourteen hours a day. Typically we started the day at five o'clock in the morning and worked all day in the operating room and clinic. Then the fellow returned to the hospital to perform the evening rounds and finished about seven o'clock at night. In the early evening, postoperative patients occasionally experienced "sundowner's syndrome" in which they would become confused and do something that could harm themselves or provoke injury. One evening a hip patient got out of bed and was found walking around without the use of a crutch or a cane. The following morning the fellow described this incident to me and suggested that we consider starting our patients weight-bearing as soon as tolerated. This was unbelievable to me because I was under the impression that the first steps after arthroplasty required the use of support. How could this man walk without a crutch or a cane and experience minimal or no pain? I explained to the fellow that the healing process took six weeks and in no way could be compromised.

Some twenty-five years later, I was sitting in a conference watching a surgical technique called minimally invasive hip replacement in which small incisions are used and the patient can walk up and down the hall with a cane for support within four hours of the operation. My colleagues were quite impressed with the reality of such a happening. I recalled this earlier incident from many years before, when the patient, even in a state of confusion, proved to us that the hip implant could support a person's weight immediately after surgery. I realized I should have listened to the fellow, as he was more perceptive than I was. At the time I was so sure I was doing everything right and proper, until this occurrence, and it later left me wondering where the boundaries are. How far can we expand, innovate, and improve on what already seems a perfect procedure?

Having fellows as students in my presence also brought a new perspective to my practice. Their young and curious minds flooded the environment with continuous questions; moreover, my display of operative expertise was constantly being critiqued because I was always working in front of an audience. The fellows did not have the opportunity to study with Dr. Aufranc or have the influence of Professor Charnley, so I believed that somehow I had to translate some of the experiences, attitudes, insights, and perspectives that my mentors had given to me. As I worked with the fellows, I was constantly reminded of the awesome responsibility of a teacher. Each morning before we commenced rounds we discussed two or three articles of the important writings in the medical literature pertinent to hip replacement. The fellows described the patients' state of health and well-being, and if they did not know the patient information, I criticized them heavily and intensely. I insisted on perfection and expected each fellow to know the patient without flaw or doubt.

Other aspects of their education occurred in the operating room, and their participation depended on their degree of competency. By the end of their fellowship, they were able to complete the entire course of surgery with expertise, assurance, and confidence. In the afternoon the fellows saw my patients in the office. As they became more experienced, they saw the patient first, and then I would see the patient to review their assessment of the problem and their management of the condition. At the end of the day, we all donned our running clothes and ran two or three miles to relax and enjoy some camaraderie. Each fellow wrote a dissertation or paper on some clinical aspect of the practice data, and it was expected that each would write a suitable paper for submission to a major medical journal. Several fellows showed qualities of professional leadership in the practice that I thought could make them a good potential partner one day. I knew a time would come when I would have to choose someone to assume the helm.

I was fortunate to have fellows who all had an underlying commitment to patient care (see Figure 9). I remember making rounds one morning

Figure 9. The Joint Implant Surgeons fellows in the early 1990s.

in our unusually early hours and walked into a room to see one of the fellows sitting in a chair by the bed. The patient had developed a gastric bleed, and the fellow had stayed with the patient all night long. He had managed the problem well and had enlisted the proper consultants to ensure his patient received the proper care. I thought to myself, "He is a true physician, putting the patient first even in the darkest situation, and putting aside his personal agenda." These young physicians gave me confidence in the future of medicine. I am sure that these enduring qualities have prevailed in this group of surgeons.

CHAPTER 10

Home and Family Life

Where we love is home—home that our feet may leave,
but not our hearts. —Oliver Wendell Holmes

I continued to finish at the office around four o'clock in the afternoon, so that I could get home in the early evening and have time to spend with our boys. We had purchased our first house, which had been built in 1834 on a twenty-seven-acre property outside of Columbus. We thoroughly enjoyed ourselves playing basketball in the barn room, playing football or baseball in the yard, riding the tractor or horses, and playing with the cats and dogs. We would go to the creek to throw rocks or just talk. There are no words to describe how much I enjoyed being with these boys.

Everything was beginning to come together. My practice was growing, and I was glad I could enjoy a meaningful practice even though the local orthopaedic community still had not accepted me. For the most part I felt very fortunate. As my schedule continued to fill, I became more stable financially. I had in place a structured program for paying off my loans and began to have some money left over, so I started down the road of material consumption. I began to spend money in a way I never had before. I felt that I had worked hard and denied my family and myself a number of things for many years, and now I was going to have it all. With this attitude, I bought a new automobile, which was a replica of the old Studebaker Avanti. It was a beautiful chocolate brown car with a sporty look to it. But when I drove it into the doctor's parking lot, it was as if I had thrown a tomato on the wall of the hospital. I asked myself the question, "Why should these practitioners be critical of the kind of car I drive?"

I took good care of my patients, I was competent in the operating room, and I had a pleasant personality, why should I be ostracized because of my car? What was missing in my mind was the fact that I was part of a staid profession, one of service, one of caring for the broken and hurting, the sick, and the dying. It was not a world where profiteering and glitz and fanciness should be displayed at the expense of another's misfortune. I did not realize that my behavior should remain within the conventional boundaries of the profession. Until the very end of my career, I fought this image issue. As I look back on it, I do not think I did anything harmful in my indulgence, but it certainly provoked criticism at the time.

When the boys started school in the local public school system, they were bright fellows and I was very proud of them. I fostered the idea that they would go to a private school in Columbus. The result was endless driving from one end of the city to the other, so again we went looking for a house. Although I still had a lot of debt, I was making money and it looked as if I was a good credit risk. We found a very special house, a stone manor near the private school. As we drove up the long winding lane to the top of the hill, we saw a beautiful home with a panoramic view of pastures, barns, and a split-rail fence (see Figure 10).

I was awestruck with this home. It was very special and its appearance was timeless. But how in the world could I afford it? I talked with my financial advisors and they said it was a risky endeavor, but if I wanted it, I should go for it. Kelly was enthusiastic about it, and again she was very tolerant of my desires and of me. I wrestled with the enormous responsibility of the price, but I began to rationalize that we would live in this house forever, I would be motivated to work hard because I had something to enjoy and pay for, and it would be a beautiful home for my children and grandchildren. So off we went to sign the papers. We moved into the house and lived in some parts of it because we had sparse furniture. Occasionally we went to the thrift store and chose furniture that was well used but had character and, within a year's time, we were fully integrated into the house.

We had lived there for a few months when a lawyer came and offered a significant profit on the house if I would sell to him. I wrestled with the idea because it was good business to sell property for a profit, to accumulate money that I could put toward my debt. But no, I wanted to keep that house, and so I declined the offer. I was committed to this farm, this house, this family, this wife, and it was the foundation on which I could continue to base my growing practice of orthopaedic surgery.

Figure 10. The stone house.

I looked forward to the weekends, which were spent mostly with our boys, traveling the property, doing various activities such as shooting guns, riding horses or four-wheelers across the countryside, and climbing the hills. I would throw the football to them, telling them about their Uncle Bill who was a great college football coach, their Uncle Dave who was an outstanding football player, and their dad, who played the game and was just "okay." I loved the camaraderie I developed with them before they reached their teenage years. Kelly would look out the window and see her beloved menfolk playing ball and enjoying one another. I also enjoyed mowing the grass, playing with the dogs, swimming in the pool, and staying up at night watching our favorite television programs in the woods in a little shack that we built to one side of the big house. These were happy days with my boys, and it was a joyful time for our family.

Kelly and I decided about this time that we would not have any more children of our own, but we would like to have more children in our midst. So we volunteered for foster care. The children came from all parts of the county, and most came from poor families and environments of neglect. They would stay for a while, we would feed them and love them and care for them, and then they would leave. We cared for one child whom no one ever came to claim. He stayed and stayed. A year went by and finally the social worker said that no one would be coming for Charlie;

did we want to adopt him? Kelly and I contemplated this decision, prayed about it, and then decided we would adopt him. So now we had Scott who was eight, Buck who was six, and Charlie, our adopted son, who was one and a half.

The effects of motherhood had made a tremendous change in Kelly. Her gratitude for the blessings we were enjoying as a young family moved her to pursue an intent relationship with God. She developed a friendship with a neighborhood couple who held a weekly Bible study. She told me about the topics and subjects she was learning and the biblical standpoint, and many of the issues were bothersome to me. Shortly thereafter I witnessed a patient's death, and I began to consider my own mortality and the existence of God in my life. I had particularly liked this man, and he had suffered greatly after the surgery. I was called to his bedside late one afternoon; he looked so peaceful as he lay there. I became aware that some day that would be me. Although in my youth the idea of my own mortality was hard to accept, when I still had a lot of life ahead of me, one day I would have to go down the tubes like everyone else who walked the face of the earth. So then I began to think about dying. I really did not know what it all meant. I suppose I was thinking that I did not ask to be born, I did not know where dying came from, although it seemed a part of a natural event. It perplexed me and bothered me. Despite this introspection, I continued to pursue my ambitions.

As my practice grew and I began to have money to spend, I did not know how to manage the cash flow. I had never taken any courses in college or medical school that advised how to manage a business. We bought things as fast as we could spend the money: new furniture, new clothes, new cars, trips, toys for the kids, and gifts for our families. We gave to our parents, to the church, to the schools; just a bonanza. Eventually the wolves came knocking at the door, men dressed in business suits who called themselves advisors. People with "deals" and opportunities to make zillions!

I remember attending an orthopaedic conference in Florida and overhearing some of my colleagues mention a character from New York who sold paintings that could be depreciated for tax purposes. I was making enough money by then and thought this sounded logical to reduce my personal income tax. I called this dealer, he came to Columbus, and I bought a number of art pieces with the understanding that they could be written off. The trouble this got me into was enormous. It soon became obvious to me that I was participating in a fraud, and I became the subject of an audit. I was placed under criminal investigation for fraud and tax evasion. I was scared. I had no idea what it really meant to be indicted for tax evasion. My attorney secured a tax attorney who got me out of the criminal section and into the civil section of the court system, and then we commenced a long legal battle that extended over five years and cost a tremendous amount of money. This experience, both painful and costly, taught me a valuable lesson, and I had to start thinking of myself now as a businessman as well as a practicing orthopaedic surgeon. I am constantly reminded of the lack of business training, and the acumen I did not have a chance to develop, during my years of education as a physician. This is a serious deficiency that is still a fact in the medical curriculum. If a doctor is a poor businessperson because of his or her own naïveté, money issues can very quickly get out of control.

Our social life changed with the acquisition of the big stone house on the hill. We were introduced to a new set of friends associated with the sport of foxhunting. I already had acquired a horse and was riding occasionally around the area. One afternoon two riders approached me. They were members of the hunt and asked permission to hunt on my property. I conceded, as a good neighborly gesture, and when they invited me to ride during a fox hunt, I took them up on the opportunity. I joined the hunt on my non-hunting horse. I felt truly out of place; my horse was very nervous and I was in the wrong attire. I felt as though I had been invited to the grand ball but was wearing all the wrong clothes.

The foxhunting sport attracted an interesting group of people. Most of them were relatively affluent, of independent means, and lived a rather casual, deliberate life of leisure. I enjoyed socializing with them because the conversation was always light, the food was terrific, and the drink was plentiful. The presence of abundant alcohol again brought the temptation for me to imbibe. I had always had to struggle with the power of alcohol, but now I set a limit on how much I would drink. When I reached that limit, then I said no to the next offer. Still we had many good times and acquired some very dear friends.

The point of this discussion about our social life is the awareness that it raised regarding the importance of community in the practice of medicine. Often a practitioner can become submerged in his or her world of medicine and fail to observe what is happening in the local community or the neighborhood. It is important for a physician to be involved in the community, whether it is in social life and civic duties or just by general participation in community events. I never thought much about that particular aspect of the practice of medicine because I was always focused on passing a test, qualifying for boards, hustling to do rounds and care for the patients, or participating in scientific circles. However, personal life, social life, the life around the domestic fires, all became more important to me as I grew older. Some of the most enjoyable times I can remember were spent on horseback, galloping across beautiful hunt country and gliding over fences; it was a thrill to experience. Diversion from the practice is important because the stress relief it provides is a prerequisite for gaining the psychological stamina required to continue in the practice of medicine.

CHAPTER 11

Episodes and Occurrences

Man is made so that he can only find relaxation from one kind of labor
by taking up another. —*Anatole France*

By the age of forty, I had a firmly established practice of orthopaedic surgery, had created a successful hip center in Columbus, had instituted a
fellowship program, was a frequently invited speaker at various orthopaedic forums, and was actively participating in the innovation of
orthopaedic prosthetics. However, as my professional involvements
gained momentum, they required more of my time, and with increasing
frequency I was invited to travel to various universities and medical centers to teach, lecture, and demonstrate. This offered the opportunity to
improve my surgical skills and expand my knowledge base, but it meant
less time at home. This speaking schedule especially killed the weekends
with my family, and I would start the workweek already tired from traveling. I struggled for months to try and find a balance between work and
home-life schedules, but the work schedule necessarily prevailed.

The patients continued to come, and in large numbers. I also began to
see patients with Very Important Person (VIP) status, and I found the
VIP patients among the most difficult patients to treat. They would have
a large influence in the community of Columbus and beyond. The challenge that these patients presented was the enormous amount of service
and personal care they expected from the system. They tolerated their state
of confinement to a certain degree, but they soon would regain their sense
of importance. The typical VIP patient ran the gamut from the athlete to
the celebrity, from the politician to the very wealthy patron. I often remembered what a senior orthopaedic surgeon said to me one day during my

residency. He said, "Thomas, I wish you well as you start your practice. May you always take care of people who have only one bathroom in their house."

What a true statement! I remembered the early days when most of my patients came from rural Ohio. They had a faith in my expertise that empowered me to give them the care I considered best for them. Caring for them created a feeling of comfort in me, I found, because they trusted me. When my schedule became busier, and the notoriety and successful momentum of this new surgical procedure brought the VIP patients to my office, the doctor-patient relationships I developed with these people were very different. I used to say that everyone was important, but some people actually were more important. Every physician who is truly honest knows that taking care of wealthy, demanding people is extraordinarily stressful.

Another difficult patient type included the physician, or a member of a physician's family. It is unusually challenging to be a doctor's doctor. I remember one patient whose son was a physician. The physician and his family in good confidence had placed their father in my care. The hip replacement surgery went well, but a few days later the man dropped dead in the hospital hallway from a massive pulmonary embolism. The blood clot traveled to his heart and his brain, and when I was called to his side, he obviously was dead. We tried everything to revive him, but to no avail. When I went out to see the family, they were cold, ungrateful for my efforts, even angry with me, as if I had been the cause of his demise. I do not know which is worse, the grief at a patient's death or the feeling of personal guilt, or whether it is an appropriation of feelings and relationships, but I struggled with these emotions when I encountered an angry patient or an angry family. In some situations, maybe, the problem might even have been my fault, but certain people have an unreasonable level of expectation. I am not certain who is responsible for the notion that all things can be made better by the great healing art of medicine.

I learned to accept that I could not perform miracles and keep everyone happy all of the time, but gradually I found myself beginning to practice more defensively and more impersonally. I watched what I said prior to the operation and made sure I kept appropriate patient records and consent forms. I maintained a distance from my patients. Gone were those early days when the relationship between us was personal and filled with love and compassion. I became a man of few words in the patient room, simply accepting that it was most important for the patient to receive a good operation, that he or she progressed well without complication, and that I could then move on to the next patient.

I remember doing rounds one morning when I asked an obese patient to walk around the room to evaluate his ability to go home. We had verbally reprimanded this patient several times concerning his addiction to tobacco and its effect on his recovery, and he had told us that he really would try to quit smoking. As he slowly walked around the room that morning, we heard something hit the floor, and we saw that a cigarette lighter had fallen from one of his fat folds, perhaps even his buttocks. I calmly bent over to pick up the lighter, handed it back to him, and stated quietly, "I think you dropped something."

It was sad that I became more of a technocrat than the personable physician I once had been, but I learned that the growing litigious nature of the doctor-patient relationship made it a tentative relationship at best, which could dissolve at any time. I perceived that my value was the capacity to perform the operation safely and allow the patient to proceed unencumbered by complication or setback. I tried this approach for a while and, not surprisingly, I began to experience more unhappy patient encounters, which tested my emotional fortitude. For example a young Vietnam veteran who had become a drug addict and an alcoholic came to see me. He had avascular necrosis of the femoral head in both hips related to his addictions. Because of his severe pain, I performed the hip replacement surgery in spite of his young age and poor health. He developed an infection in one hip, which I treated, but it persisted. He went to another doctor who was able to treat the infection successfully. Meanwhile, he sued me for mismanaging the infection. His lawyer was a brash and obnoxious individual who, during the trial, asked me if I had prayed with the patient. I answered in the affirmative and emphasized that it was by mutual consent. The lawyer called me a religious fanatic and told me I should have been paying more attention to the medicine and less attention to the praying. This degrading admonition insulted me, because I had worked very hard to solve this patient's problem. This episode was a test of my faith because I felt betrayed by my patient. For quite some time I remained mad at the patient, the lawyer, and at medicine in general.

Other doctors referred many patients to me. A female patient, similar to many, came to me because of a loose implant. She had previously undergone numerous operations and was quite debilitated. She told me that she desperately wanted to have her hip replaced again. During the surgery I discovered major bone destruction in her hip. As we prepared the area, I inadvertently slipped an instrument over the top brim of the pelvis and cut an artery. Blood quickly filled the wound and she was near death before we could repair the vessel. She survived the surgery but never recovered from the trauma. She remained hostile toward me and sought alternative orthopaedic care. The fact remained that we had the good fortune to save her life despite this occurrence.

A prominent Columbus businessman who had a total knee replacement and several revisions developed an infection. I took him to surgery and successfully eradicated the infection by washing out the wound and removing his prosthesis. However, he was left with a flail, unstable leg. In an attempt to restore stability, we fused his knee. He became reinfected and the infection spread throughout his lower leg, eventually requiring amputation. As these experiences occurred, I became more calloused and indifferent. I was trying to maintain my sanity in the face of the enormous impact that undesired results would have on my practice. It seemed as though everyone was angry with me, leaving me disheartened by the burden of the stress.

I pondered my patient care program, and I realized I had to accept that I was doing my best and that not everyone would have an optimum outcome in spite of my greatest efforts. I rededicated myself to following my Christian faith, and I consciously attempted to schedule more time for recreation in an attempt to avoid burnout. I threw myself into the horse hobby with enthusiasm. A foxhunting friend told me about a game called polo. The idea of a game on horseback was intriguing. I had heard about polo and had seen a match on one occasion, but I had never attempted to learn about the sport. I discovered that some very enthusiastic polo aficionados lived in the Columbus community. Some from the foxhunting group were joining the polo club, so I decided to watch a match to see what it was all about.

I became fascinated with the game because its strategy is very much like the game of soccer. The horses are beautiful, usually small, wiry thoroughbred types. They go for eight intense minutes in what is called a chucker, and there are four to six chuckers in a game. The players wear helmets, boots, and white chaps, and they swing a long stick with a mallet head to hit a ball about the size of a baseball. I joined the club and began to play the game regularly (see Figure 11). As with most other

Figure 11. Tom Mallory riding Flipper at a polo match.

endeavors in my life, the more I played, the more absorbed in it I became. Sometimes my enjoyment of the game seemed to replace my love for medicine. I went to work, but I found I was thinking constantly about the next polo match. I began to buy good horses, and I hired a groom and a professional player to help me learn to play the game. I began to spend more time on the polo field and less time in the operating room and at home. At first I played on Friday evenings or Saturday mornings, then I added Sunday afternoons, and then Wednesdays as well. It provided such a relief from the stress of my practice that my new passion was starting to get the best of me. I was concentrating on polo at the expense of time with my family and patients.

Meanwhile I was having a great time. I was getting better at playing the game, learning to ride, ride fast, stop, turn, and hit the ball. This was a great group of people in terms of macho men. Many were in their middle age. We traveled all around the state of Ohio, to Cincinnati, Dayton, Akron, and Canton, and occasionally to Lexington, Kentucky. I spent the weekends playing polo, and it took a serious toll on my marriage and family. I started getting heat from Kelly for missing church on Sundays and for being unavailable to spend time with the family. She was right. But my love for the game blinded me at the time, and I continued to pursue and enjoy the polo events with all the enthusiasm I could.

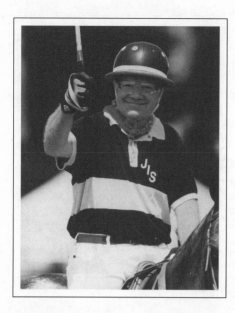

Figure 12.
Welcome to the
patients' polo picnic!

I had been playing polo for about two years when I suffered my first major injury. My horse turned suddenly, and I lost my balance, fell off the horse, landed on my shoulder, and broke my collarbone. I was scheduled to leave the next day for a speaking engagement in Sweden to demonstrate my surgical technique. I remember feeling the bones grate together as I worked in the operating room in Sweden. I began to reconsider my commitment to polo. The game was dangerous, and in reality it was very trivial when compared to the value of my family and profession. Following this recuperative period, I limited the time I spent on the polo field but continued to play the game for some fifteen years.

My patients always were interested in and excited about my love of polo, so the office sponsored an annual patient polo picnic in the fall, and it was well attended by many of my patients and their families. I arranged for teams of polo players to come and play for this special audience, who enjoyed watching their doctor ride up and down the field playing with his team. The matches were exciting and the atmosphere was filled with friendship, complemented with good food and drink. These events always were special occasions (see Figure 12).

As I put the polo experience into perspective, I must admit I had a tremendous amount of fun. Polo is a grand game, and I always felt my athletic appetite satisfied by the endeavor. I enjoyed the camaraderie with other players and the spirit of game and sport that was so renewing and refreshing. The diversion relaxed me and helped me to look at other aspects of my life from a fresh perspective. In my mind I never aged; I always was twenty-one years old when I was playing polo. I used to think I would play polo forever, so it is no wonder that I miss the game. Maybe someday in heaven I will get to play polo again.

CHAPTER 12

The Orthopaedic
Manufacturing Industry

"Doctor, what's your price?"

Since the initial conception of total hip replacement first appeared, the search has been ongoing for the ideal design and materials for a durable hip implant. Charnley's concept of low-friction arthroplasty was revolutionary. It consisted of a small stainless steel ball articulating or rubbing against a polyethylene or plastic cup, and fixed to the bone with methylmethacrylate cement. The materials, though durable, were subject to wear and therefore finite in their life span. Most surgeons who studied with Charnley were convinced that his prosthetic design was perfect and would never need changing. He was consistent in the use of his prosthetics and his long-term results were remarkable. Others who followed his surgical techniques had similar results. However, in the later 1960s, when the prosthetic concepts were introduced into the United States, innovation commenced immediately. The first major modification involved changing the size of the femoral head and changing the configuration of the stem portion. The polyethylene acetabular cup remained unchanged at that time.

As my practice continued to grow, I became a significant user of implants. At the time the choice of prosthesis was left to the discretion of the surgeon, who was therefore in a position of influence, wielding tremendous economic impact. Initially I was extremely naive as to the impact of my practice, not only on the economics of the hospital but also on prosthetic revenues for the orthopaedic prosthesis manufacturing companies. The large volume of implants used in the hospital did not go unnoticed, and even the presidents of companies began to cater to me.

They would fly in on their company planes, take me to dinner, expostulate on the value of their particular company's offerings, and express their hope that I would consider using their company's hip products. The realization began to dawn on me that I would create a bias if I selected a prosthesis on any basis other than what was best for my patient. When I selected a company, economic incentives were offered to reimburse my willingness to use their prosthesis, to promote it, and to advise them of its efficiency and effectiveness. The pattern of reimbursement at that time was commensurate with any consultant's role in the profession or in a business at large. Initially the compensation was reasonable and appropriate, but it eventually became excessive.

During the total hip replacement procedure, bone cement was applied to the canal of the bone. To prevent the cement from running too far down the canal, a plug (also made of cement) had been developed and was distributed in a small unit that was premixed, applied, and allowed to set before the larger batch was mixed and placed to fix the femoral stem. The procedure was slow and not very efficient. A sales representative for the company whose implant I was using attended surgery with me frequently, and, although his job was to manage the inventory, provide assistance with implant selection, and serve as a liaison with the orthopaedic manufacturing company, he asked me if it would be possible to put a piece of plastic in the canal instead of the plastic plug. It sounded like a great idea to me. The sales rep returned to his company, suggested the notion, they manufactured the plastic plug, and we began to use it. The plastic plug worked extremely well and saved fifteen or twenty minutes in the operation. It was easy to insert, it was consistent, and it did not move when pressurized as the cement was injected for the femoral stem. It was a true home run; little did the sales rep or I realize that, had we patented the plug idea and design, we would never have had to worry about our financial well-being ever again!

Some time later while I was traveling in Europe I noticed this plug was being used everywhere. Soon other orthopaedic manufacturers were offering a similar product; it became the gold standard procedure to confine the bone cement to the proximal femur. Later I published my clinical results using the plastic plug, and it since has been acknowledged as one of the significant contributions to the technology of joint replacement surgery.

I began my venture into product innovation and development with Joint Medical Products, a relatively new company in the industry that was struggling to distinguish itself. The bioengineer for this company was the most creative and most industrious person I had ever worked with, and he was intrigued with the concept of modularity. Modularity in joint replacement surgery would allow a surgeon to customize a prosthesis in terms of length, size, width, offset, and various other features to restore anatomy to a patient's joint right at the operating table. Additionally, the idea also allowed for a worn or broken part to be replaced without dissembling the entire component.

Meanwhile researchers everywhere were looking for an alternative to bone cement. The proposed alternative was a porous surface on the prosthesis that would allow bone to ingrow, which could be achieved by a tight fit of the prosthesis in the bone canal, thus avoiding the use of cement. So we began attempting hip replacement without cement, but in my opinion the femoral component design was a challenge. I was fascinated with a new concept in which the femoral prosthesis was in the shape of a wedged taper instead of cylindrical. The purpose of the stem was to bear the load through the joint and transfer it gradually across the bony surfaces of the femur. If the load-bearing or weight-bearing forces were too concentrated in one area, the patient would feel thigh pain. A tapered stem fit the upper femur in concert with its anatomy of various geometries. When the taper design first appeared, however, it was considered revolutionary but still tentative and yet to be proven.

The next step was to test the concept, and although laboratory tests can support a technological advance, they do not always represent conditions within the human body. We proceeded with the stem design, and I began to use it in a clinical trial period. What do you say to a patient when you are trying to test a prosthesis whose design is yet in question? I took considerable time to explain all of this to the patients, and they signed a form to participate in the experimental study with informed consent. We also applied for permission to implant the test prosthesis, through various review boards at the hospital, ensuring that our motives were known to be the advancement of the profession through good practice. In all my days of practice, I never felt that I took advantage of a patient by trying to innovate or change some of the problems that arose with an implant design.

The subsequent development of a hip system was serendipitous. A phone call to William Head, an orthopaedic colleague from Dallas, Texas, revealed that he was working independently on an acetabular component, which could complement my stem design. Dr. Head had preceded me by

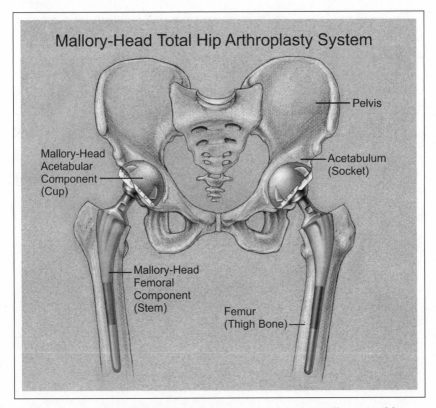

Figure 13. An illustration of a hip replacement using the Mallory-Head hip system. Drawing by Joanne B. Adams.

one year as an Aufranc fellow in Boston and remained on the faculty at Harvard for several years before he returned to his hometown. After he returned to Dallas, he began to develop a joint replacement practice similar to mine and was very busy and productive. His acetabular design incorporated the use of fins to secure the fixation of the shell to the pelvis so that bone ingrowth could occur. We were musing about the features of both components when it became obvious that he had what I needed, and I had what he needed. We proposed that the components would work well together. Our system would feature bone-ingrowth technology to avoid the use of bone cement, use of bone strut grafts to replace bone loss, and a calcar prosthesis that had the capacity to manage most general and specific hip replacement problems. The combination of my stem design and his cup design was introduced by Biomet, the company that Dane Miller founded in 1983, as the Mallory-Head hip system (see Figure 13).

Dr. Head and I promoted this system around the country and the world. Dr. Head was a very effective speaker and an excellent teacher. We traveled extensively to lecture on our prosthetic concept and to promote its design, application, and use. Dr. Head continues to lecture on the orthopaedic speakers' circuit about the outcomes of the Mallory-Head system. This system continues to prove effective with worldwide use.

CHAPTER 13

The Orthopaedic Speakers' Circuit

Almost every man wastes part of his life
attempting to display qualities that he does not possess
to gain the applause he cannot keep. —Samuel Johnson

In my lifetime I have given hundreds of presentations to orthopaedic surgeons around the world. Not only did I have no formal training in the art of public speaking, my only credentials were that I had performed numerous hip replacement operations. I had one distinct advantage in the orthopaedic field, which was that I was in the game early with joint replacement technology. Many of the topics I presented were based on my personal experience and offered a subjective observation. As the field became more complex and sophisticated, more surgeons participated, however the content of my presentations now included observation along with the patient follow-up. The lecture halls at various meetings were packed with orthopaedic surgeons who attended the conferences to hear the latest developments on total joint replacement technology.

Over the years, despite all the verbosity and rhetoric, the basic tenets of joint replacement have not changed. How could you improve on something so spectacular? Many speakers prevailed simply by giving entertaining presentations with editorial comments on what already was accepted as established technology. Nothing was perceived to be so boring to an audience as the monotonous presentation of data. Moreover, meaningful data was hard to generate because of the clinical variances that existed. I learned early in the business, as a speaker, always to show X-ray examples and to present follow-up examples, even if the follow-up was of short duration. Even within a short time frame, a trend would usually become apparent and, when observed, would answer some of the questions as to whether the innovation was relevant or just incidental. Participating in the presentations became for me an exercise in human discourse. I learned I had to be quick of wit and nonspecific in my statements because the criticism was exacting if a casual or off-the-cuff remark was made.

The orthopaedic speakers' circuit was also a way of becoming known in the field, and the only way to survive was to "dance on your feet." I could never anticipate a question, and it was impossible to prepare beforehand. A working knowledge of the subject and the ability to conceptualize and articulate the answer was the best response.

Early in my career I was asked to participate on a panel with Charnley. He was so bright and so experienced that no one in the room could ask a question that could really stimulate him. Many practitioners who asked questions were not really thinking, they were just talking. I realized quickly that if you do not have anything to say then it is better to keep your mouth shut. In addition, it is important to think in terms of questions, not answers. A good question is worth a hundred answers. It provokes critical thought and allows validation of the speaker's capacity to disperse meaningful information.

I enjoyed being part of the orthopaedic speakers' circuit, which offered interesting conversation, hearty meals, good libation, and enjoyable camaraderie. Some of my closest and most valued relationships with colleagues were generated in these surroundings, as was the case with Dr. Larry Dorr, who practices orthopaedic surgery in Los Angeles, California. He had invited me to a seminar he was hosting. At the seminar I learned that he had invited me to be on stage as if I was on trial. He badgered me with questions and challenged me with concepts. I really think he had trouble fathoming the depth of experience I had to offer at that time because I was deeply involved in the orthopaedic technology. I handled his queries and probing questions with grace and ease. He insisted that I go to the operating room and operate on one of his patients. The surgery went well, and at the end of the operation he spoke directly to me: "Tom, you are a good surgeon." The tone of his statement was as if the realization came as a great surprise to him!

Dr. Dorr commenced an annual Masters Series in which he selected ten or twelve surgeons from various parts of the country to come and demonstrate their operative techniques in surgery filmed live and transmitted to an audience of orthopaedic surgeons. It was critiqued by surgeons who were looking to learn just one more move, one more nugget of information, that would make them just that little bit better, a little more efficient. To be a demonstrating surgeon on Dr. Dorr's faculty was a prestigious position, and I felt honored and fortunate to be selected as one of the initial surgeons to participate. My assignment was to operate using the Mallory-Head hip system on an elderly patient suffering from osteoarthritis of the hip. It was an exciting event, although I was aware of the hypercritical environment. I knew I needed to be prepared for the best execution of the proposed operation, so I arranged for my personal scrub nurse and my PA, Doug, to assist me. On the day of surgery I arose early, exercised, said my prayers, and went off to the hospital confident that no one was more prepared or competent at this surgery than I was. I knew that Dr. Dorr would bombard me with questions and challenge my capacity for knowledge.

About halfway through the operation, when the femoral component was ready for insertion and the cement was setting, I noticed the handle was stuck on the instrument we used to insert the femoral component. I placed the femoral component in the canal, allowed the cement to harden, and then tried to remove the instrument from the prosthesis. It would not release. A bond had been created between the driver and the component. It essentially was dry welded to the driving platform handle. After a long period of effort, we finally were able to disengage the device with a hacksaw. It took an enormous amount of time, and so to my embarrassment the moderator decided to close the broadcast from my room and go to the next surgeon's demonstration. Upon checking back later, the audience found us still trying to cut the instrument from the stem. I thought my performance would leave the impression on the entire audience that Tom Mallory was mediocre at best, subject to problems in the operating room, and most unimpressive.

My ego was shattered. I had gone to Los Angeles totally prepared to be the best and had walked away looking like the worst. Dr. Dorr was very tolerant and chuckled because the problem was eventually resolved. Once the instrument was cut away, the patient had no ill effects from the operation. Later I learned that the experience actually was considered beneficial to some in the audience, and my work had been interpreted as an exercise in problem solving in the operating room. It was a very humbling experience, but I was challenged to return in a year to perform a more difficult operation, a revision hip surgery that involved the exchange of a failed prosthesis for insertion of a revision calcar femoral component. And this time I was ready for anything and everything.

I opened the thigh from the hip joint to the knee, danced through the soft tissues, extracted the failed prosthesis quite easily, and inserted the femoral component perfectly. The hip was reduced to its normal position, the wound was closed smoothly, the skin was stapled together, and the response was outstanding. Compliments included "best operation of the day." A year earlier I had felt a complete failure and had received a poor response to my performance; now I was greeted with adulation and appreciation, and I felt a sense of accomplishment, achievement, and satisfaction. Again I was reminded of the enormous contrasts in the life of a surgeon: thrill, risk, danger, opportunity, glamour, success, discouragement, and failure.

As I returned to Columbus from Los Angeles that year, I was reminded of the similarities between surgery and athletics. The dexterity, the tension, the preparation, the anticipation, and yet the unknown result of the game or event or operation all left one suspended in a world of risk and responsibility. Such a life holds the possibilities of an intensity that can be realized only by those who assume the role and accept the challenge.

I was fortunate in the subsequent years of demonstrating my techniques in the Masters Series always to have good results. I was full of confidence and was heralded as "the surgeon's surgeon." Through all my days of orthopaedic surgery I wanted to be reckoned one of "the best," and maybe just for this moment I was almost there. Coming off such a high or such a low as I have just described is stressful either way. However, this Master Series provided some of my moments in the sun, and I have no regrets.

CHAPTER 14

On the Home Front

We cannot always build the future for our children,
but we can build our children for the future. —Franklin D. Roosevelt

Watching our three sons grow up in the stone house on the hill was a highlight of my middle years (Figure 14). We were a happy group. We enjoyed travel and went to various places in the United States and abroad. The boys were good children, and they brought little grief to Kelly and me. They became athletes, and Kelly and I followed their athletic careers with enthusiasm. Academically they were solid. I can reflect on the boys' growing years with a sense of pride that I was a caring and concerned father although I often was delinquent on physical presence. I had my own standards as to what I thought these boys should be: independent, responsible, and capable individuals. I wanted their academics to be solid and their brains stimulated, and I encouraged them to be driven to do something and be somebody.

To that end, when they were each twelve years old, I started to send them to summer camp. The boys hated to go to camp because they were attached to their home and their parents. Each June we waved as they boarded a plane taking them to Camp Kiwanis or Outward Bound, or some other experience in Colorado. We missed them greatly, but they always came home a little tougher, a little more secure in their own sufficiency and capacity. It made them more aware of the great privilege they had to be loved and cared for by their mom and dad. This entire endeavor was wrapped in concern for their Christian faith. I encouraged and participated in church activities and attempted to model as best I could the things I was advocating.

Figure 14. The Mallory men: Grandpa, Tom, and sons.

I made sure the boys had jobs even when they were young. The job situation was predetermined for them. I found people to hire them at an early age who would help them learn to work. For example, I paid a carpenter and blacksmith, a kindly person and a Christian believer, to hire Scott when he was twelve years old to be a gofer. Kelly packed him a lunch, and he would go off to work, spending the day carrying boards back and forth to his carpenter mentor. To this day Scott refers to that job as one of the most rewarding experiences of his youth.

Bucky worked with the car salesperson at a dealership when he was fourteen or fifteen years old. This was a special arrangement, because I was one of the best customers of this car dealer. Bucky was unaware that I had arranged for him to be paid through the dealership. His experience started out as "the doctor's privileged son" and finished as "one of the gang." He was a hard worker and gained the respect of the employees on his own. Both Scott and Bucky profited from their early work experience, and I believe the moorings of their successful businesses were established during those early years.

Attempts to find jobs for Charlie were not so easy because he was an independent spirit and chose to do his own thing. Many times his own thing amounted to watching television instead of working, which frustrated me. But I came to realize that you can only push a person so far and then their response is one of rejection and hostility.

I took each boy to the hospital at some point in their teenage years, hoping that one of them might want to become a physician. Each of them accompanied me on morning rounds, viewed a case or two of surgery, and went to the office. Not one of them showed a positive response that indicated an interest in medicine. In fact, two of the three passed out, embarrassing me immensely as they lay on the floor and I tried to revive them, and finally I had to carry them out of the hospital. It was obvious they did not want to be physicians.

My relationship with Kelly was strained from our lack of personal time together. We still loved each other, but as the boys grew, the demands of my schedule and her duties trying to fill both mother and father roles created little time for intimacy. At that time I viewed my marriage as utilitarian. Kelly was well cared for in terms of well-being, clothing, cars, home, and so on, and although I was frequently absent she knew I was supportive. We divided the responsibilities of the home, but my communication skills were lacking.

My involvement in the game of polo was an additional stress on our relationship. I believed that polo was my thing, my time, that I had worked hard to meet all my obligations and deserved to have a fascinating hobby. I felt justified that I tried to involve Kelly, but she was not interested in polo and chose other activities such as raising our children. We were professing Christians, committed to be faithful to our marriage, committed to avoid divorce, and we had a basic belief that we were secure together. I continued to play polo, and Kelly became more frustrated with my preoccupation. Being an independent sort, she soon developed her own social life, and as I continued mine we grew progressively farther apart.

One weekend I arranged to go to Lexington, Kentucky, with Scott to play polo. We left on a Friday and came back on a Sunday. I learned later that Kelly had gone unescorted to a couples party. She was a very attractive woman in her early forties, and I knew that she was vulnerable, and I was as well. I realized her behavior was a reaction to my frequent absences while playing polo, but I did not like it. I immediately cut back on playing polo. I selected games that were closer to home, so I was there more frequently, but I did not stop playing altogether. I made more of an effort to improve our time together, but the distance in our relationship continued for many years.

One day I was listening to some audiotapes on marriage as I drove home from work, and the essence of the message was that a husband should cherish his wife. This word "cherish" hit me like a bullet in the chest. Here was the problem. I had not cherished Kelly. I had assumed that she knew I loved her and cared for her, but I did not cherish her or nurture her feminine nature. I decided that from this time forth I would spend the rest of my days loving and caring for Kelly, being concerned about our relationship, doing my best to cherish her. I hope that perhaps I have managed to do so, and I can honestly say that this effort changed our lives around. We went on to have a blessed marriage. In our later years, we have become very close and devoted to one another.

Meanwhile the boys grew up and went off to college, excelled, and began their adult lives, which was a great source of satisfaction for Kelly and me. After the boys went to college, the stone house on the hill felt very empty, so we decided in 1988 to move into a quaint little section in the downtown metropolitan area of Columbus called Sessions Village. We bought a little cottage house, leaving the stone house behind without regrets. We just drove down the road and left the place where we had raised our boys and spent fifteen great years together.

CHAPTER 15

The Entrepreneurial Quest

Man's mind stretched to a new idea
never goes back to its original dimension. —*Oliver Wendell Holmes*

Many physicians are oblivious of the monetary activity they generate within a practice. As a surgeon develops and matures in the profession, there are two mind-sets: the first is one of acquiescence, and the second is one of entrepreneurial spirit. The physician who chooses to acquiesce stays within the confines of the medical practice and becomes subject to the institution or the system. The surgeon who has an entrepreneurial spirit chooses to gain control, ownership, administration, and development of the goods and services that he or she provides. Those who acquiesce are satisfied simply to practice medicine and are fulfilled personally and professionally in their physician role. However, the entrepreneur remains largely dissatisfied with the current position while enduring constant stress to manage the process of health care not only from the perspective of the doctor-patient relationship but also from that of a hospital, business, or commercial enterprise. I chose the second mind-set, and I did all I could to develop and manage the business aspect of my practice. My choices led to many encounters with the business world. I always felt at a disadvantage because I had not been trained as a businessman, but I realize that hard work, good service, communication, and continual awareness of my practice were all essential elements that drove my practice to its success.

An example of budding entrepreneurialism was the recognition that many would come and observe our patient care system and incorporate the system features in their own practice.

Visitors came from elsewhere in Ohio and from all corners of the world. They brought their questions and their curiosities, their insights and their concerns. From their feedback, I sensed they were impressed with the organizational format, the fact that we ran from two to four operating rooms simultaneously with a senior surgeon performing in all four operating rooms. As I look back now, the practice was indeed remarkable, but it was orchestrated so that the main part of the operation always was under my direction. The enormous number of patients coming through the system (up to fifty at a time in the hospital) was handled efficiently because of the appropriate delegation of responsibility.

What always perturbed me, however, were those visitors who would come, watch the system in process, glean observations from the surgeon's eyes, then go home, initiate these same rights and activities, and then take credit for their origin. Few ever thanked me or acknowledged the fact that their ideas of practice management were formulated after a visit to our center. I believed the information should be dispersed freely to help improve patient care, so my problem was not a lack of wanting to share the vision. Even to this day I am consoled that these systems were beneficial to so many thousands of patients. What bothered me was the absence of gratitude, the lack of acknowledgment or credit.

I never thought much about the office environment I supervised although I have been told that my office was the epitome of efficiency. I remember a good orthopaedic friend telling me that the office should be a place for evaluating the new patient for their need of a total hip replacement, and for the rest of the patients it should be a place for celebration. He was right, because when hip replacement surgery is done well it offers such consistently good results. So, as a practitioner all one really must do is apply the operation when the diagnosis is appropriate, perform the operation with skill, and celebrate the results with the patients. This philosophy worked well for me most of the time. But the averages always took their toll, along with the disgruntled patients. I would say the group with complications and unhappy encounters comprised 5 percent of my practice; the other 95 percent of patients were happy, appreciative, and loyal.

In 1986 the office was moved to a convenient location on the corner of a busy boulevard in Columbus where some forty thousand vehicles pass each day (see Figure 15). A sign displaying *Joint Implant Surgeons* not only identified the building but also served as a reminder that we were a community institution. The traffic flow in and out of the large parking

Figure 15. Joint Implant Surgeons, office, 720 E. Broad Street.

facility was easy. The office was welcoming, with a large and gracious reception area and friendly reception staff.

We had a large, open office space with twelve patient rooms. After the patient was taken to an exam room, the first person to see was the nurse clinician, then the resident, the fellow, and finally me. I did not spend a long time with the patients because by the time I arrived most of their questions had already been answered. However, I tried always to be sincere and genuine, and to deal with their major problems. If it was a postoperative visit, I congratulated them on the success of their hip and gave the credit to them instead of taking it upon myself. I credit much of the success in the office to the many talented nurses who worked for me. These nurses had a genuine compassion for the patients that is seldom seen in other professions I have witnessed. I made sure my patients did not have long waiting times; we had a rule in our office that patients should wait no more than twenty minutes before seeing the doctor. Despite many attempts to enforce this rule, it was hard at times to make it prevail, but nevertheless, our intentions were good and generally our patients were not inconvenienced by too long a wait. All employees were expected to conduct themselves in a professional manner, all were well dressed, and the men wore ties with their white coats.

The pace was quick, the environment was personable, and the atmosphere was upbeat. The nursing staff spent the morning doing telephone triage, answering patient questions, and conducting continuing care over the phone. We would see from thirty to sixty patients in an afternoon, beginning about one o'clock and finishing by half past four. We had two X-ray units running continuously. We were extremely service oriented, no patient ever was treated with intentional disrespect, the environment exuded education and facilitation of the operation we proposed. If anything created a delay, it was analyzed, dissected into parts, and rebuilt into a model that ensured continued efficiency. I kept a scrapbook full of letters of appreciation for services rendered by our mutual efforts. It was indeed a source of rewarding and sustaining acknowledgment of what we had done for people.

Clearly the system worked. Perhaps it could be packaged and marketed. One concept would be to outsource the management of the orthopaedic service to an entity that would assemble the infrastructure and manage the joint replacement center independent of the hospital. This system offered the opportunity to hire specific medical and administrative personnel and staff to satisfy the physician cadre. We were in the process of moving to a new hospital, so we proposed to the administration that we would manage our own orthopaedic service with the idea that we would reach certain economic quotas. These quotas would create enough revenue for the hospital to be comfortable and pay the management fee for outsourcing the administrative function surrounding the operation of the joint replacement center.

With the new management system in place, I was able to choose my own nursing administrator, patient care advocates, and physical therapist, and I was involved in the specifics of the day-to-day operations through these management people. We evaluated our service with the use of patient questionnaires, and for the most part patients were very satisfied with the service they received. Moreover, this also allowed us to improve on hospital inefficiencies by addressing issues that encumbered the smooth execution of the service. The model functioned well in our setting. Therefore, we decided to package the management system and create an entity called Med Center Management. The Med Center Management model was made available for other practitioners to use in their sites with the basic concept of outsourcing orthopaedic care to a management company within a hospital system. This was quite a novel idea and was evaluated by a number of centers around the country. The challenges were obvious. If we had the right people in the right place, the model worked very well; but if we did not, then the inefficiencies so characteristic of the hospital environment would reappear and were left uncorrected. This example illustrates that it is possible to innovate when the entrepreneurial spirit is vibrant.

By this time the practice was getting beyond my capacity to manage as a solo practitioner, however, so I began to look for an associate to help me. Where better to look for a partner than among the fellowship group that was passing through? I hoped I could find someone compatible, who was capable of someday coming to the helm of this large practice I had been so fortunate to develop. Former fellow Adolph Lombardi Jr. came to mind. He was very loyal, and he was committed to the continuing success of the practice. Subsequently he and I managed the practice together, and he helped my caseload tremendously. He was a hard worker, and he took on the more difficult revision cases that were so time-consuming on the surgery schedule. One advantage was that his coming to the practice left me more time to spend with my family and on other activities.

Around this time we acquired a small farm near my brother David's farm in rural northern Ohio, which we could use for a weekend retreat. The hills were tranquil and beautiful, the place was isolated, the atmosphere bucolic and quiet, and it was here that I rested after the long tiring days of medical practice. Kelly and I began to enjoy the rural home and farm so much that going back to the city on Sunday evening was always a sad time. I began to think I could have a life again, in the country ambiance, living on the farm and commuting to Columbus a few days a week.

This idea restructured my whole working mind-set. Dr. Lombardi was becoming ever more efficient and effective. He was developing into an outstanding knee surgeon, and he demonstrated the capacity to handle enormous workloads without flinching. His administrative skills were being honed as he prepared to assume the day-to-day management of Joint Implant Surgeons so that I soon could live in the country and have a limited practice. I had always figured I would practice medicine up into a ripe old age and that I would be capable and effective for a long time to come. I had reached the pinnacle of hip surgery in terms of capacity, and it was hard to keep the surgery interesting because I had done it repeatedly for so many years.

I started to lose some of my capacity for speed, efficiency, and effectiveness. On one occasion I fractured the femur as I put the femoral prosthesis in place. I never had struggled with that particular aspect of the operation before. Observing me with interest, as he always had done,

Doug was particularly sensitive when he expressed his thoughts that perhaps I was losing my skill set. I responded angrily, forced all the nurses to come into the operating room to watch me as I performed a demonstration hip replacement, making all the moves to a degree of perfection that I had in fact given up a long time ago. Having been subject to their direct and indirect criticism, I used this demonstration to emphasize that I still had the capacity to be the best. From that day until I retired, I do not think I fractured another femur or left anything behind of which I could not be proud.

CHAPTER 16

When Systems Fail

*Success is the ability to go from one failure to another
with no loss of enthusiasm.* —*Winston Churchill*

A man came into my practice for advanced arthritis in both knees and needing bilateral total knee replacement. He also had peripheral vascular disease, which was a risk factor in major surgery, but he was evaluated by the internist, and he passed the screening for vascular integrity of his lower extremities. I performed simultaneous bilateral knee replacements. The surgery went well, the procedure only lasted a couple of hours, and the patient's postoperative course was uneventful. Later that evening he complained of pain in his legs and numbness in his feet, and it was thought that prolonged analgesia from the anesthesia was contributing. The anesthesiologist reacted to the symptoms by regulating the epidural medication the patient was receiving for pain control. The nurse who made rounds at nine o'clock that evening examined the lower extremities and found them cold and without feeling. In addition, the muscle strength in his legs was weak, so she called the anesthesiologist who reduced his pain medication.

Early the next morning the third shift nurse, who had checked the patient several times during the night and had found his condition unchanged, could not identify pulses in the feet. The orthopaedic team assembled for early morning rounds and confirmed that the patient's feet and legs were cold, numb, and weak. I received a call that the man had an occluded popliteal artery. I rushed to the hospital to find the situation serious. When the vascular surgeon arrived, he examined the patient, diagnosed the vessel occlusion, and emergently took the patient to the operating room to perform popliteal bypass surgery. The patient had a rough postoperative course and continued to deteriorate. The end result was amputation of the lower extremity just below the knee.

Needless to say, the family was upset and accused me of neglecting my patient's postoperative course and of irresponsibility in supervising my staff. The consequence was an enormous malpractice lawsuit that resulted in a settlement of colossal proportions. I was distraught. I had established a system of checks and balances and a team of personnel to monitor the course of each patient so that things like this would not happen. I had allowed the systems to operate and for the most part, day after day, they were effective. However, on this one occasion the system had failed, which resulted in the amputations, the lawsuit, and the award. Although the tragedy was not of my doing, ultimately I was held responsible.

It was hard for me to rationalize this occurrence. I knew I had done the right thing by having the systems in place; I was hurt by the fact that the consequences were so tragic. Again, I reiterate how painful malpractice incidents were in my professional career. Their tendency is to make one cynical and to promote the practice of defensive medicine, ordering more and doing more than necessary in order to accomplish the therapeutic imprints, simply to protect oneself against frivolous lawsuits. There is no such thing as zero risk in the elderly when performing joint replacement surgery. The mind-set that I maintained through my thirty years of practice was to enjoy my patients for they had brought the world to my doorstep. I enjoyed the excitement of the surgery that I performed for each patient and that brought so much benefit, but knowing problems could occur at any moment made me like a woodsman, always listening for sounds—sometimes real, sometimes imagined—that might warn me of a predator.

From this time forward, I had difficulty obtaining malpractice insurance coverage. I had practiced joint replacement surgery with major success for thirty years, and now I stood at the front door of the malpractice insurance office pleading for coverage. When legal awards of this dimension are made to patients, the awards are recorded in a permanent database that tracks the incidence of malpractice as well as the amount of the award granted. This constitutes a malpractice history for the practitioner and enables the insurance to favor those physicians who operate less or who fill their practice with a low-risk patient population.

I staggered out of this experience quite cynical. My defense attorney was a great support and encouragement to me, and I will always be grateful for his words at that time. He counseled me for many hours, encouraging me not to give up at this stage, to continue to practice medicine regardless of this tragedy. Like all the storms I had weathered in the past, I grew from the experience and gleaned a certain sense of wisdom about the vicissitudes of life. All the patients who experienced flawless surgical outcomes after their operations were less memorable than the man with the monstrous tragedy of the amputation. My Christian faith helped me immensely during this time, providing strength to avoid negative thoughts that could lead only to depression and ruination. I finally was beginning to function again with some sense of confidence and capacity when I made the decision to step down and allow Dr. Lombardi to assume the leadership position in the practice.

Part 3

Lessons
Learned

CHAPTER 17

Being Fit Was Always Fun

The greatest wealth is health. —*Virgil*

From an early age I have always exercised and pursued physical fitness. I continued to find great relaxation in running long distances, but in retrospect I see that this probably was not a good choice of exercise. Running consumed a lot of my energy, which already was dissipated by my hectic surgery and travel schedule. The mileage added wear and tear to the arthritic knee that had developed from my injury in high school. I ignored its weakened state, however, and never thought it would become severe enough that I could not run. I continued to enjoy the emancipation that running afforded from the moans and groans of everyday life in the office. At the end of my running career I had competed in five marathons (see Figure 16). Although I never claimed to be very good or very fast, I always went the distance and finished the race.

My final marathon was the New York Marathon on Sunday, October 28, 1985. This took place in New York City, and it was a beautiful day, one of those crisp autumn days with a bright blue sky filled with fluffy white clouds. Doug and I arose early and went to the location for the runners to assemble for the race. More than ten thousand runners gathered as the race began. There were so many competitors enlisted that it took twenty minutes for us to cross the bridge to the starting line.

Doug took off running at a brisk pace. I soon fell behind him, but I ran a steady pace. I noticed the crowds gathered in enormous numbers on either side of the street, encouraging the runners with their cheering. I had never seen New York more cordial. It was an exciting event. The race seemed endless, but I did not feel the pain, only unevenness as I

Figure 16.
Tom Mallory
running the race.

tried to keep my feet flat on the ground. The streets were in deplorable shape. They had been resurfaced with asphalt numerous times, creating an undulating, rolling, wobbling surface geometry and contour. This persistent irregularity made it very difficult to run. The course went into Harlem and then toward Central Park. At one point I looked over at the crowd and recognized one of my former fellows. We called him Woody, and he was one of my favorites. As I ran near him, he pointed to one runner and I observed a large scar on each of his knees. I ran up alongside the man, commented on his knees, and he told me that he had undergone two knee replacements, one of which had become infected. I could hardly believe it; he was younger than I and was running a marathon on artificial knees. I wondered if he realized how injurious running was to the implant patient. I told him I was an orthopaedic surgeon, had performed many knee replacements, and that I was quite concerned about his running on the implants. He replied, "Doc, it does not matter. I am living for today." I often wonder where the man is now, and what price he paid for such foolishness.

I have thought about that race many times since. It really was not so much a race as an experience. Like so many things in life, the race depends upon persistence and endurance. At that time in my early fifties, I was still in competitive shape for cross-country running, playing polo, weight lifting, and swimming. One day I read in an athletic brochure about the advantages of carrying weights while running, and the benefits for resistance training. I was fascinated by the idea, which created a quadruple resistance by using weights on each upper and lower extremity. I decided to try it, a running program with "heavy hands." I lost weight, muscled out, and was feeling great as I worked up to carrying twelve pounds in each hand. I felt I was truly in shape. I had a lowered pulse rate and reduced cholesterol level, and I thought I was a perfect example at age fifty-four of a healthy aging male.

Then I was advised to change life insurance programs and acquire a different policy. This process required a physical examination that included an electrocardiogram. It showed enlargement of the heart and a defective heart valve that was leaking blood. The cardiologist insisted I immediately stop carrying the heavy hands and stop the running program. He recommended a series of tests to determine whether the leaking valve was significant enough to require open-heart surgery. When I learned the results, I was devastated. Within a forty-eight-hour period my spirits changed from happy confidence to devastation, my self-opinion from what I presumed was good health and optimum conditioning to being, in my mind, a cardiac invalid. This episode represented a benchmark, a life-changing event for me. Hereafter I would deal continuously with health problems, to a greater or lesser degree, and ultimately I found my life redirected into a completely new sphere.

My initial reaction to the cardiac diagnosis was that it must be wrong, erroneous; I could not accept the doctor's recommendation. I sought the opinion of several physicians and chose the suggestions that I liked best. The course of treatment I chose included cutting back on the heavy hands and slowing my exercise regimen, with the result that everything would be fine. I stopped using the heavy hands altogether, continued to run and play my equestrian sports, and for the most part continued to feel good. However, I knew that my health was defective. I could no longer assume all was well within my physical being when I was harboring a problem that could progress.

On the heels of the cardiac prognosis came a gradual hearing loss. I could no longer distinguish conversation in the operating room, and speaking engagements became difficult because I could not hear the questions from the audience. I began to make inappropriate responses and comments because I had not heard correctly. At first I was unaware of my hearing loss because it was subtle and continuous, but it soon became obvious to those around me that I had a progressive hearing deficit. This was confirmed by the appropriate auditory tests, and it was recommended that I begin to wear hearing aids. I was fitted for the aids, but they were a total disaster. They were of no help whatsoever and, in fact, were a complete aggravation. I could not hear, but neither could I stand the hearing aids. I did not want those silly things in my ears, so I struggled to hear in the operating room and lamented another physical faculty beginning to ebb.

I felt that the health I had always taken for granted was beginning to slip through my fingers. Doors were closing that I could not reopen. Heretofore most of the injuries to my body had been bruises, bumps, and fractures, all of which eventually healed. They were intense, but in time corrected themselves with only memories of the problems remaining. However, these newly diagnosed conditions meant I was changed permanently, in both these capacities. How do you react to irreversible loss? You grieve, get angry, go into denial, finally realize the condition is not going to go away, then you find a way to cope. And the degree to which you cope often is a test of persistence, courage, determination, or just sheer effort.

I had a remarkable opportunity to pursue the absolute best treatments for these health problems because of my position as a physician in the community and my financial capacities. I decided to seek the best doctors I could find, and this I did. I went to California to see the otolaryngologist who treated former president Ronald Reagan. He told me I had a hearing loss that probably was premature because of the sound environment I had been exposed to in the operating room for many years. I had used noisy, heavy drills for hours a day. He said hearing aids were the only option, and that new technology was making them quite effective. I learned there was a computer digitized hearing system, and I immediately agreed to try it. Within a short time I was hearing at a reasonable level. My cardiac status remained unchanged at the yearly interval exams, so with the hearing aids and a stable heart condition, I continued to practice medicine—somewhat marred, but certainly not defeated.

CHAPTER 18

My Three Sons, from Boys to Men

Other things may change us,
but we start and end with the family. —Anthony Brandt

Perhaps one of the most traumatic experiences of my life as a father was the Gulf War, for my oldest son, Scott, was involved in this encounter. Scott went to West Point, graduated in 1989, became an artillery officer, and was moved into the Gulf War conflict early in his military career. As the war commenced, we sat fixed to the television, and although we heard the good news that the troops were advancing rapidly through Iraq and toward Baghdad, we were fearful our son might be wounded or killed in the process.

My demeanor was melancholy as I sat watching the television, recalling many years earlier when as a young resident I first looked into the eyes of my little baby boy in the nursery ward the morning of his birth. Then I remembered Scott as a little boy and the times he, his brothers, and I would ride our horses and ponies over the countryside near the big stone house. I remembered his decision to go to West Point and his arduous years there. The years had gone by quickly and now he was so vulnerable for injury and demise. He had gone through the basic training, prepared himself as an artillery officer, and now was in the midst of a war. I was thankful for my Christian faith that was a source of solace and assurance to me through those weeks and months. I found comfort in my confidence that, despite the outcome and the consequences, Scott would be alright. And he was alright. He distinguished himself as a courageous officer and received the bronze star for his bravery.

Then we did not hear from him for months after the war ended. One day the phone rang, and we were delighted to hear Scott's voice, explaining that he had been stationed in the desert in a postwar occupational role, and finally he was on his way home for an extended vacation. When he arrived at the airport, we all were there to greet him. It was one of the greatest moments in my life, and it was as if he had come back from the grave. I often think of World War II, as well as the many other wars this country has fought, and the price many families have paid when their loved ones have not come home. I have thought about the price so many have paid that a guy like me could have a career in medicine and be blessed with so many wonderful opportunities.

My second son, Buck, also was influenced by the military life but in a different manner. He wanted to be an attorney, but the discipline of military life intrigued him. He was a quiet-spoken young man who had proved his athletic prowess as captain of the high school football team. In fact, his team was so remarkable that they reached the finals for the state championship. In his final game, the opponent's halfback sped around the corner, and Buck, who was playing linebacker, took off after him. Buck ran across the field with ferocious intent, grabbed the player by the shirt, and threw him to the ground to prevent a touchdown. I was so proud of him as I witnessed this great effort, knowing well that he had learned the lessons that create a winning attitude.

Buck's attitude was illustrated further in college when he went to marine camp for officer's training during the summer between his junior and senior years. He had some difficulty with his vision and was held back from the rest of the company out on field duty. As he waited for the eye doctor to give him permission to return to the company, he learned that he had not completed all the activities required for the marine recruits. He was badgered and harassed by the sergeant over this issue, but as the weeks ensued, he caught up and began to excel. As I sat in the bleachers on his graduation day, I was proud that he had worked hard enough to be in the top of his graduating class, and I knew that no matter what Buck did in life, he had that certain toughness that would prevail.

My third son, Charlie, passed through the high school years, but he did not find his purpose in life. No matter how much I insisted on achievement, he lacked motivation. When he graduated from high school, I gave him a car just as I had done for my other two sons. Shortly thereafter he got in the car, drove down the driveway, and disappeared. He literally lived out of the back of that car on the streets. Some time later I learned

Figure 17.
At home with
my three sons.

that he was working in a fast food restaurant in a rural community in
northern Ohio, and we reconnected. He asked to come home, and we
gave him another chance. We started down that long road again of trying to establish his capacities and encourage him, but he continued to
struggle with various issues for some time. He experienced college, married, and is now a devoted father.

As I reflect on the family and my fatherhood, I know there are things
I should have done differently. However, I was earnest in my efforts, and
we remain a close family (see Figure 17).

CHAPTER 19

A Brief Retirement

*There is something about the outside of a horse
that is good for the inside of a man. —Winston Churchill*

I tried to spend most weekends on the farm as it was an idyllic location. It afforded quality time with our family and we all enjoyed the serenity of the setting and the outdoor atmosphere. We drove away each Sunday evening after an enjoyable weekend wondering what it would be like to live at the farm full time. In the summer the rains come heavily and the thunderstorms are numerous in northern Ohio. One June night in 1987, a bolt of lightning struck the log house and instantly set it afire. Within a couple of hours, it had burned to the ground. The farm is so isolated, no one noticed the fire until it was too late. My brother Dave called to tell us the house was gone.

I remember going through the smoldering rubble and ashes at the bottom of the house where the fire had occurred. Only charred remnants of our former possessions were still evident, and one of the objects that I noticed was the wood-burning stove. The intense heat of the fire had not destroyed it. As I was looking at the stove, a familiar object in the corner caught my eye. As I walked toward it, I recognized the toy bulldozer that had been given me so many years ago in Boston, the bulldozer I would need to move the rock. It was scarred and burned, but I brushed it off and it was still intact. I took the bulldozer to my home in the city and placed it on the mantle where it could be viewed because it symbolized so much of my past.

We wondered what we should do to replace our weekend abode. In 1988 we built a small cabin down the hill from where the log house had

142

sat, and we used this as our weekend retreat for several years. We loved the country so much that I considered changing my life to spend the rest of my days in the country with my family. Kelly was enthused about the idea as well because she loved to garden, cherished her privacy, and enjoyed painting with oils. The setting was perfect for a tranquil retirement. We decided to enlarge our existing cabin to make this our permanent home.

The new house was unique because of the techniques and materials used in its construction. The living room was paneled with wood imported from Farnwell Hall, a manor house in England. The manor house had been disassembled and the wood from one of the studies was transferred to an antique dealer who sold the paneling to us. The wood was reconstituted and assembled in the living room walls by an English craftsman, and to this day it remains a stunning accomplishment. I have never entered the room without feeling a sense of history.

Since the house was completed, many special memories have been generated. I frequently recall Christmas Eves spent by the fireplace in my comfortable chair with reflections of the fire and the Christmas tree lights dancing off the walls. The happy voices of my grandchildren will forever be ingrained in the spirit of this special house.

It was around this time that my brothers and I (see Figure 18) had to make some decisions about our aging parents. My parents were teachers who retired comfortably and lived a tranquil life. Their demise was rather traumatic, however. One day my mother walked into the house ahead of my father and, assuming that he was inside the garage, lowered the garage door. The door struck him on the shoulder, knocked him to the ground, and caused a pelvic fracture. He was taken to the local hospital where he was treated supportively with traction. After lying in bed for four or five days, he began to deteriorate. I was out of town on an orthopaedic lecture tour, but when I returned I had him transferred to a trauma center in Columbus. The traumatologist proposed a plan to surgically repair the pelvic fracture, anticipating that it would improve his ability to move and address issues of personal comfort. However, his condition worsened during the hospital stay and he developed lower lobe pneumonia. Because he was considered a poor surgical risk at eighty-seven, he was treated with immobilization and transferred to a convalescent center. He continued to deteriorate and then expired about three weeks after the initial injury.

I remember the last time I saw him; I knew that the end was near. I kissed him on the forehead and walked out of the room, then turned

Figure 18. The Mallory brothers: Bill, Tom, and Dave.

around and looked back over my shoulder. I could not help but remember the many fireside chats we had shared. I hoped I had met his expectations, but somehow now it did not matter.

Mother continued to live independently for two years after my father's
death, and then at the age of ninety she moved into an assisted living
facility. Several years later while she was in the hospital for an infection,
she suffered a severe stroke and was placed on life support. Her stroke
was extensive, and it was obvious she was seriously impaired and little
could be done for her. The three brothers again agreed that no heroics
would be extended to Mother; we would let the condition run its course,
and if she were stable we would admit her to a convalescent center. Her
plight drew the family to her bedside; the grandchildren visited frequently
and engendered optimism. One night I received a phone call from one
of my sons who said he had visited with his grandmother. She awoke
briefly, called him by name, and then fell back into a stupor. He said that
all the grandchildren wanted to give her a chance to make it and requested
that we not "pull the plug." I shared this plea with my brothers, who
concurred, and a feeding tube was inserted. She lived another year, but
her quality of life was vegetative. She was placed in a nursing home near

my residence and I would go over in the evenings to feed her. The nursing home was filled with patients with Alzheimer's and other degenerative conditions. I looked around and heard the moaning and groaning, coupled with furrowed faces. Mom would sometimes turn and scream with pain from the prolonged periods of immobilization and inactivity. In my mind I spoke to her, "Yes Mom, they call me Chief, but I am unable to help you now. I tried to help you when you first had the stroke, but when they put in the feeding tube, it simply prolonged the inevitable."

I looked at Mom and remembered all the things she had said to me and the things she had done for me. I still felt her maternal force, and I recalled all those years of her great effort on my behalf. I thought especially of the faithfulness of her monthly financial support during my education, how it was all she could give at the time, and how it helped me achieve my goal in medicine. I thought of her optimism, her tremendous power of engagement, and her sense of expectation. She always believed in what I was doing. I knew that I never could have been the Chief without the help of Mom and Pop.

I was becoming more absorbed in the future I had in the countryside. It seemed to me as if it would be a perfect place to just fade away after years of practicing medicine. Horses, rural scenery, and so many other intangibles were providing great comfort and enjoyment to me. On my workdays I would come home early in the afternoon and ride my favorite horse, and while I was riding, my thoughts were a long way from the operating room. I knew my days in practice were numbered. Dr. Lombardi had by now assumed the helm. He was leading the charge with competence, and I was satisfied to retreat to the farm, happy to spend the rest of my days in this manner. But this contented view of my anticipated future fell apart when I received a phone call from one of my business colleagues who informed me that I had been named a candidate for chairman of the division of orthopaedics at the Ohio State University.

CHAPTER 20

They Call Me Chief

The most effective teacher will always be biased,
for the chief force in teaching is confidence and enthusiasm. —Joyce Cary

I had spent nine years at the Ohio State University for my doctorate of medicine and my residency training in orthopaedic surgery. To think that now I was considered a candidate to chair the orthopaedic division was beyond belief. You can understand some of the sentiments of pride, excitement, and fear that were vibrating in my mind. I realized it was more than just a passing thought when the dean called me to schedule a meeting.

The dean was an engaging individual, bright, assertive, and progressive in her thinking. She had experienced the medical education world in various diverse roles as practitioner, researcher, teacher, and administrator. She explained that she was aware of my career and believed there was no need to search outside Columbus for someone to lead the OSU division of orthopaedic surgery. Until this time orthopaedic surgery had been a division of the general surgery department, along with several other surgical specialties at the University Hospital, but now the university wanted to expand this specialty into a department of its own and develop subspecialties within it. Two objectives were of utmost importance in filling the chairmanship. First was development of a department that required both substance and structure. And second, it was the intention for Ohio State to acquire a small hospital on the east side of the city for the purpose of creating a center of excellence in orthopaedics. This proposition comprised a big vision and an immense dream, and the dean assured me, "You are the man for the job, Tom, you can do it."

I replied that I would consider the offer and left the meeting. I was wondering about how much this episode was like my overall career. I felt I was too old, too tired, too cynical to be the kind of visionary leader they needed. It seemed an impossible job to develop wholesome medical practices in an offbeat small city hospital setting. University medicine is different from private practice. The practitioners in an institution-driven entity are subservient to the institution and its mission. Little or no room is available for entrepreneurs or the entrepreneurial spirit. The system is static, it feeds on itself, and it perpetuates its own sense of security by controlling change. Somewhat like government, the university system does not vary, it has its own personality and its own force, and individuals within it do not change it. The Ohio State University was no different from any other institution. It remained a magnificent school with a grand history and a distinguished record of graduates who had gone on to successful careers. But to create an orthopaedic center in such circumstances would indeed be a tremendous challenge.

As I was riding my horse along the trails of my farm, I realized that if I took this position I would spend my remaining energy trying to accomplish the goals that were set. Did I want to finish this way? I had acquired a certain amount of wealth that could sustain me, I had a beautiful home and an enjoyable lifestyle in the country, and I had been looking forward to a slower paced, more leisurely life. Why would I want to go to the university and assume that difficult job and all the stress it would entail when I had just been relieved of all that stress in my private practice?

I realized, however, that there are jobs, there are positions, and then there are opportunities. The chairperson in a university setting has enormous influence and control over his or her section of medicine and becomes the barometer by which the environment is measured in terms of its educational intensity. The multifaceted aspects of education spread out from the undergraduate to the graduate, postgraduate, and even into the community. One could say that the chairperson is responsible for developing the culture or the environment in which education occurs, not only for the resident pursuing a career in orthopaedic surgery but also for the undergraduate or medical school student rotating through this section of medicine. This educational responsibility would be enhanced by the presence of a research program, conferences, outpatient services, and the interrelationship between the medical school and the local and national community. It was an awesome position, and it was unbelievable to me to think that this position was being offered to me—after so many years of being considered a renegade, a peripheral factor, a rebel with only a self-serving cause. Was I qualified? I did not think so, but obviously someone thought so, and the position was offered to me. My thinking at the time was that this was an unprecedented opportunity. I would regret it for the rest of my life if I did not take the chance to establish an orthopaedic surgery program, a center of excellence.

I believe that if you live long enough you realize that nothing comes without change of circumstance. The community had finally changed its attitude toward me. I had practiced long enough and well enough that my record was transparent. I certainly demonstrated deficiencies, I did not contest that, but I also had valuable strengths. Apparently the community was willing for me to assume the chairmanship mostly because I was local, knew the orthopaedic community, and would involve the community properly within the teaching envelope of the university.

Kelly and I spent many hours discussing whether I should take such a big step at this stage in my life, and how it would affect her and our marriage (see Figure 19). Again, Kelly was supportive of my decision, and I decided to give the job a go. I thought I could meet the goals, get the door open to the new orthopaedic center, and stabilize the department. I anticipated that this new journey of mine would last several years, and in the meantime I could teach the residents and fellows and could choose the cases I would operate in the University Hospital. I planned to maintain a dual citizenship, one the professor and the other the retired veteran surgeon.

As I drove onto the Ohio State University campus on the first day of my chairmanship, the medical center complex stood before me. I drove up the long ramp into the parking garage. There were hundreds of students, teachers, and support staff in a human quagmire. My confidence was running on empty. What was I doing here? Not for one moment did I feel I could manage this situation. I felt like turning around and hightailing it back to the country. Instead I persevered, parked my car, grabbed my briefcase, and started down the ramp. I heard someone say: "There's Dr. Mallory, the new orthopaedic chairman. That's a tough job."

Once at the task, I saw that obviously many changes were needed. The first was to recruit a staff of practitioners to represent each of the different specialties. I saw two options: one option was to hire surgeons from outside the community, bring them in, set them up, and let them compete for patients against the already existing orthopaedic community; the other option was to identify surgeons in the local community with

Figure 19. Tom and Kelly, anniversary celebration.

well-established practices who were also qualified to teach. If they were willing to bring their patients, their practice, and their experience, it would be a win-win situation for the university and the surgeons, and we could very quickly build a faculty that was reputable and productive. The immediate revenue-generating activity of these established practitioners served to sustain and increase the capacity of the orthopaedic department to grow and improve.

Meanwhile, the dean of the medical school became ill and resigned. An interim dean who was supportive of our program served until a permanent replacement could be found. After establishing the resident teaching format, I realized there were flawed attitudes, practices, and activities that created an unacceptable environment. I perceived the residents to be uninspired. They lacked a vibrant dynamic passion for learning. They appeared to be simply sliding through the residency to orthopaedic practice without a sense of purpose. This observation was confirmed by an encounter with one resident. One of the first operations I performed as chairman of the department of orthopaedics was a knee replacement on a farmer from the northern part of the state. The resident assigned to the joint replacement service was a pleasant chap, a good-looking person with a nice personality and friendly appearance, but he was ill prepared. He knew nothing about the patient, did not know any of the history of the illness, and had little or no knowledge of the history of knee replacement, its evolution, development, indications, or applications.

I demonstrated the surgery to him step-by-step and gave him a good basic core of information on the procedure. Later in the day I returned to visit the patient on the floor of the hospital and asked the nurse, "Has the resident been in to see the patient?" The nurse answered, "No, he has not and he is unavailable. He took the weekend off to visit his parents in Philadelphia." I learned later that weekend that he had not arranged for any coverage of his service while he was away, which further added to my dismay.

When the resident returned from his trip, I had a long conversation with the young man. I explained that his responsibility toward the patient at his level of education included a working knowledge of the patient's problem, a concept of the rehabilitation and therapy proposed, and an understanding of the postoperative course of the patient. I warned him of the serious consequences if he was poorly prepared for the next patient.

When the next patient came along, he repeated the same performance. He did not have knowledge of the patient or the procedure and did not participate in the patient's postoperative care and course in the hospital. So he faced the consequences. I fired him for three days and told him to get out of the hospital, to go home and think about whether he really wanted to be an orthopaedic surgeon. He was shocked. He returned a changed person and, for the rest of his residency, was conscientious and involved. In retrospect I really believe he was testing my authority and wanted to validate who I said I was.

Throughout my life I had been highly impacted by good teachers and practitioners who stimulated my curiosity and encouraged my intellectual development. I made a concerted effort to spend time with the residents individually; and when I got to know them, I found that most of them were somewhat naive. They were serious about their education. It was obvious that they had spent a lot of time and money to get to this stage of maturation and were for the most part serious about becoming competent orthopaedic surgeons. I perceived, however, that they did not feel a call to a great cause, and I felt very disturbed by this observation.

I encouraged the residents to find a special interest and to pursue a fellowship or postgraduate year after their residency at Ohio State, to explore the opportunity to excel and to realize their potential.

I felt strongly that this residency program should encourage residents to pursue excellence and become people of character. I asked them to consider their core values and the effect of those values on the doctor-patient relationship. The usual format was for me to meet the residents very early in the mornings to make rounds, discuss topics regarding joint replacement, and then proceed to the operating room where I would spend most of the morning teaching the intricacies of surgery. I would have them come to the office and see patients with me, and I tried diligently to model some of the characteristics of my mentors and the traits that they had modeled for me.

Once we had established a relationship, the residents were very responsive. It was as if they were my children and I was directing them through a chaotic world, giving them a sense of reality. One thing I wanted to encourage was their sense of the larger orthopaedic community that exists beyond Columbus. To this end, we had the opportunity to host a group of orthopaedic residents and trainees from the Asian and Pacific basin. These young physicians came from Japan, Korea, China, the Philippines, Australia, and New Zealand (see Figure 20). They were sponsored by the American Orthopaedic Association, and the duration of their stay was approximately one week. During this time, they participated in our educational seminars and gave presentations to our residents and faculty. The weekend of their stay we had a grandiose event up at the farm and staged a polo match. I played along with my groom and several other polo acquaintances. It was a highly contested game and near the end of the match, one of the horses slipped, fell, and broke a leg. We procured the services of the country veterinarian who used a mobile X-ray machine to reveal an inoperable fracture. The horse had to be euthanized. The whole experience left a lasting impression on this younger generation of orthopaedic surgeons. The question obviously was one of curiosity. Why could the fracture not be fixed, and the life saved? Why was the only alternative euthanasia? Perhaps in this generation of practitioners, someone will cross a boundary and develop a way in which animals too can benefit from the technology that has been generated through the current orthopaedic community.

The main emphasis of my time with the residents was spent in surgical training. I took them through each part of the joint replacement operation that I had done for years. I felt very comfortable with this because

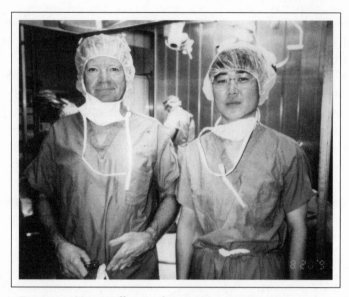

Figure 20. Tom Mallory and an Asian visitor.

I had mastered most, if not all, parts of the surgery, and they easily followed and reproduced my steps. Together we gave the patients a good
operation and at the same time each resident enjoyed the advantage of
learning the steps and their proper execution. Moreover, the patients
knew that we were working together as a team; they understood they were
in a learning environment in which a certain portion of their operation
would be performed by the resident staff, and they were assured that I
would not abandon the patient to the resident.

The junior residents rotating on my surgical service participated in the
surgery from an observation standpoint, watching various stages of the
operation and asking questions about the various anatomical structures
and procedures. One day I was moving rapidly through the dissection of
the hip to enter the joint when a resident stuck his finger in front of my
knife. I did not have time to retract and I amputated the tip of his right
index finger. He bellowed with pain, fell back, and collapsed to the floor
as blood gushed from the finger. I broke scrub, applied pressure to his
hand and controlled the bleeding, then quickly arranged for him to be
transferred to another hospital where a microvascular surgeon replanted
his fingertip. His convalescence was prolonged, painful, and difficult. He
eventually regained use of the finger but the tip remained numb. He fin-

ished his orthopaedic residency with essentially a nonfunctioning index finger on his right hand. He appeared to compensate well from the incident, but the event left a serious reminder of the dangers in the operating room, not only for the patient but also for the surgical team.

Of all the many venues, activities, and adventures that I had experienced as a physician and orthopaedic surgeon, I can say that none was as exciting as being the chairman of the Ohio State University orthopaedic department. The fact that I had a chance to influence the practice of orthopaedics in a broader scope was very humbling. I recall all the good mentors I had: my parents, teachers, patients, friends, colleagues, family, wife, and children. What a way to leave a legacy! It seemed as if the opportunities of the job were endless and I was being consumed by it, but I felt that it definitely was worth whatever price I was paying to create a culture that had been such a big part of my life. The acting dean called me in one day toward the end of the academic year and was excited to tell me that the senior medical students were being matched to the various residencies they had sought. He complimented me that fifteen graduates of this medical class had decided on orthopaedic surgery as a career, and they had acknowledged their time with me as a factor in their decision.

On the personal side, the job was taking a tremendous toll on my home life. On the days we did not stay in Columbus, I was getting up very early in the morning and driving the hour or more to Columbus, then spending a very busy day with my own patient practice in addition to all of the responsibilities and demands of the chairmanship. Although Kelly was supportive, she also was feeling the stress. Our life was extremely fragmented. On the weekends when I was home on the farm, I had so much to do, but I was tired and needed sleep. As the days passed I began to feel weaker, as if something was creeping into my body; I just was not the same old Tom. I knew the cause at the university was valuable, but I also realized I was over sixty years of age and that I was working extremely hard. In the back of my mind I kept thinking something might be wrong with me physically, but I had learned in my early days of football to suck it up and go on; I tried, now, not to let my aching, fatigued bones slow me down.

However, I continued to fatigue easily and experienced progressive weakness, to the point that every task was taking more and more effort. I noticed in the operating room that I was having trouble holding the cauterizing instrument called a Bovie pen. I just could not make it work. At first I thought it was a defective Bovie; I would push against the button on the side of the cylinder that energizes the cautery with little result. I even thought that perhaps I should get a foot-activated device because I could not make the hand control work. Moreover, when I did make it work I could not keep my finger on the button long enough for it to do the dissection that was needed. What was wrong with me? What was happening in my body? I could not figure it out. I assumed I simply was working hard and pushing myself to a point of fatigue and, with a little rest, everything would be fine. I continued to persevere with my busy schedule.

The dynamics surrounding my university position were interesting. The opportunity for developing an orthopaedic center of excellence, where the majority of the procedures were musculoskeletal in nature, was the driving force in my acceptance of the chairmanship. The physical setting of the hospital needed further renovation. The proposed plan was expensive and beyond the capacity of the existing budget. The board of trustees decided not to pursue the renovations. I was assured that the situation was temporary, but I was frustrated that the board had not grasped the vision that I had. I pointed out that the concept of an orthopaedic specialty hospital certainly was not new, and that I had made it successful at St. Ann's Hospital many years earlier. Furthermore I told the administration that this model had proved effective in Germany and the United Kingdom for years. But the concept of the center of excellence was postponed, much to my disappointment. I began to realize that my dream of a stellar orthopaedic center was not going to happen during my tenure as chairman. During this time my arthritic knee condition worsened, and I decided to undergo a total knee replacement.

CHAPTER 21

Now the Patient

The mask is removed.

What is it like to be on the other side of the knife? I pondered this question as I anticipated my own total knee replacement. I recalled many complications that I had observed as a surgeon and that I had managed in my own patients over the past thirty years. Although serious complications are rare, a total knee replacement is a major operation fraught with danger, pain, suffering, and occasionally even death. The knee ligament I tore many years ago on the football field had predisposed my knee joint to degeneration. Such an injury would now be surgically repaired immediately and the stability of the knee restored. Most likely the outcome would be more favorable, and the deformity and arthritis I suffered later would not have occurred. However, I had come to the point of total replacement because I had neglected my chronically unstable joint. I am amazed how insensitive I was, as a practicing surgeon, to my own knee condition. I am reminded again of how quickly we become old and how slowly we become smart. I should not have been running marathons, nor should I even have pursued football in college. I should have managed my weight and exercise regimens in ways that would specifically have avoided additional damage to the knee.

My decision to have a knee replacement was based on the increasing pain and deformity in my right knee. As I promoted total knee replacement as a treatment alternative to my patients, they in turn would ask me, "When are you going to have your total knee?" The deformity, dysfunction, and pain finally became unbearable, and I decided to proceed with the surgery.

In preparation for surgery I sought an environment that was safe and successful, just as I had done for my patients. The elements included the right surgeon, hospital, anesthesiologist, internist, and support systems. I was anxious about the control I would lose when I went under the care of my surgeon and the hospital medical personnel (see Figure 21). The rigid routine of the hospital would prevail, but the operating room and floor staff would be watching how I handled my pain and circumstances. Did I dare complain? How would I manage anxiety and apprehension, not to mention the pain after the operation? Should I go with the flow and mix it up with the other patients, or should I seek exclusivity, go for a private room, and isolate myself? How quickly would I regain control of my postoperative course when it was my own operation? I soon found all of this out as I scheduled the total knee replacement for early January 2001.

The day of surgery has become somewhat of a blur in my recollection. The surgery went beautifully, performed by my colleague Dr. Lombardi. He is an excellent surgeon, and I knew he would do a very good job for me. Moreover I knew he had a steady hand, seldom got rattled, and was able to handle the tension of operating on me. I was scheduled to get out of bed that afternoon, but I could not because of the anesthesia and analgesia. The following morning I was able to stand, but it was no easy task and was quite painful. Gradually I acclimated to the process and by late afternoon I had improved significantly. But as the anesthesia wore off, I was in a state of nausea and pain. The nausea was persistent and was associated with natural gastrointestinal dysfunction. The postoperative swelling subsided and the blood clot around the knee began to dissipate as I did the physical therapy. The exercises were painful initially, but as the swelling continued to subside, I had much better movement in my knee, which improved my flexibility and comfort.

Then I developed dysentery. My medical consultants diagnosed it as an antibiotic-induced colitis. The diarrhea continued for some time, I lost twenty pounds, and my strength ebbed. And now I was bothered by the fact that I was no longer the physician in charge. Doctors do not stop being doctors when they are patients, and the treating physicians care for the physician-patients differently from their other patients. Because the relationship is awkward, compromise can occur, and in the process the best medical judgment is not always exercised. I was learning very quickly that a process was occurring in my life that would humble me, break me, and completely reorient my attitude toward health care and patient proficiency.

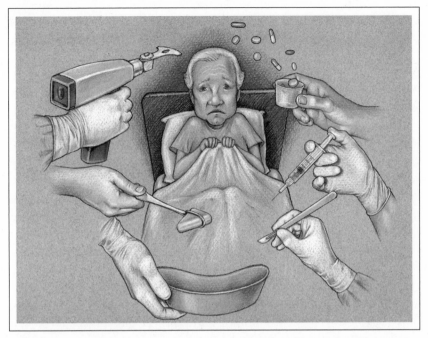

Figure 21. Tom Mallory, now the patient. Drawing by Joanne B. Adams.

After a two-month convalescence, I returned to my duties as chairman and continued to practice joint replacement surgery. But even after getting back into the routine again, I knew something was definitely different. I experienced relentless fatigue; I did not have the dynamos running in my engines that I once had, no turbo speed. I would drag through the day, falling asleep in a chair midafternoon when I paused for a few moments of rest. I noticed that my right shoulder and arm did not swing while I walked, and I had a slapping gait. Although I observed these tendencies, I passed them off as being the result of fatigue, and I did not pay much attention until I was presenting a paper at a conference in California. As I held the laser pointer in my right hand to direct the audience attention to the projection screen, my hand began to shake and I could not stop it. This was the first time I noticed that I was developing a tremor in my right hand. I immediately diagnosed myself as having an intentional tremor that seemed benign. I thought it resembled the symptoms displayed by my mother, and she had lived a very full and involved life in spite of a tremor in her hand. I thought I could still operate with competence and remain in control of the situation. I did not believe the tremor was serious, and I was quite certain I could manage it.

I am amazed now at how I isolated myself from the problem, to the point of denial. I completely justified the condition. The greater issue at the time was deciding how to manage my orthopaedic practice while functioning as the chairman of the orthopaedic department at OSU. I discussed my medical issues with several of my colleagues, and I decided it was time for me to withdraw from the academic leadership role and simply commit to my practice of joint replacement surgery with a slower schedule.

When I gave my resignation to the dean of the medical school, he asked me to remain involved in an ancillary position to support the education mission and to encourage and promote leadership among various orthopaedic faculty members. I accepted the offer and worked for several months as a liaison between the clinicians and the administration. I also continued to work with the medical students and the residents. I was amazed at how rapidly things had changed in the short period of time I was out of the department for my surgery. The university is constantly changing its protocol and compliance issues.

At my farewell encounter, I was presented with a plaque, a clock, and a T-shirt that said Chief. As I walked out of the hall with my wife on one arm and my other arm filled with medical memorabilia, I thought how much I had given, how much I had tried, how little I knew what a difference it would make in the lives of these young orthopaedic surgeons who had studied under my supervision. I did know one thing. I had been privileged to be their teacher, and it was a great honor.

I returned to my rural moorings, worked three days a week, and rode my horse in the country the other two days. It was fun. I felt as if I finally could enjoy a long and well-deserved rest, and I began to consider that I was coming to the end of my career in orthopaedics.

I was invited to speak at Seth Greenwald's Current Concepts in Total Joint Replacement course in 2001 (see Figure 22). The room was full, and although I did not realize it at the time, it was my final talk. I had been asked to speak about my experience as a patient receiving a total knee replacement, and the talk was entitled "Lessons from the Other Side of the Knife." I thought this would be a monotonous and unappreciated presentation. I talked about the athletic days and the practice years, the gradual discomfort and deformity that happened to my right knee, and finally the decision to have the total knee replacement. I described the events of

Figure 22. Tom Mallory and Seth Greenwald, lifetime friends.

the surgery and all the follow-up entailed. I finished simply by saying that it was an enlightening experience to be the patient and recipient of the operation. I went to sit down, and when I finally looked up, I could not believe my eyes or ears. They were giving me a standing ovation. Apparently, what I said, the transparency with which I described my experience, had pushed the audience to a state of identification, sympathy, and admiration. I felt truly honored. This presentation all but concluded my speaking experiences as I soon was diagnosed with Parkinson's disease.

I had often wondered, would I know which surgery day and case would be the last I did? Or would it happen like a thief in the night? As it turned out, I did not know which day was the last day. It was in January 2002. I was scheduled to fly to Buffalo, New York, the next day for a unicompartmental knee replacement in my other failing knee. I performed four operations that day and everything went very well. Even though I had the tremor, I compensated for the weakness in my right hand with other maneuvers, and I breezed through the surgery. Doug was across the operating room table that day, as he had been for the past twenty-five years. I always appreciated his comments about my surgery, whether positive or negative, and as we finished that day he said, "This was a good day, Chief, just like the old days, huh."

As I walked down the hall to leave the hospital, I encountered one of my scrub nurses. I told her I felt I was operating rather well despite my tremor. She replied that she had been concerned I might have Parkinson's disease, and to see me still functioning was a good sign that I did not have that "cursed condition." I walked out, got in my car, and drove away, not realizing for a minute that this was my last day as a surgeon. That was it. I did not know it was over, but it was.

I flew to Buffalo, New York, where an authority on unicompartmental knee replacement performed my surgery. The operation went beautifully, and I was released the next day with minimal pain. I was immediately back on my feet, and I was fully recovered within six weeks. This experience stood in stark contrast to my total knee replacement. Although this was a lesser operation, it was orchestrated beautifully, and I had no complications. However, I noticed that my tremor worsened, and I began to wonder if something else was causing this debilitation. I sought the services of a prominent neurologist in Columbus, who diagnosed me with Parkinson's disease (PD) in early April 2002.

Parkinson's disease occurs when nerve cells die in a small part of the brain. When functioning correctly, these cells produce a chemical called dopamine that directs muscle movement. Deficiencies of dopamine result in the gradual loss of muscle control. In addition, the individuals suffering from this disease demonstrate imbalance and rigidity, but mostly they present with an obvious tremor. The condition is incurable, chronic, and progressive in nature.

As I staggered out of the doctor's office, I just could not believe the diagnosis. There must be some mistake. My mother had a tremor in her later years, but she never had a Parkinson's diagnosis. I figured it to be a familial trait and that I did not have Parkinson's disease. I thought, "I will prove it. I will find a doctor or group of doctors who will appreciate the fact that I have been misdiagnosed." I began doctor shopping, but every one confirmed the diagnosis. Finally I gave up. I started to take the medicine, and it made me very sick. I felt very fragile where before I had been bold and strong. I turned reclusive and withdrew from everyone, even my family. I was definitely depressed. I struggled with every motive and purpose—I did not think I could continue the rest of my life being chronically ill. I just could not imagine it. I recognized that the Parkinson's diagnosis meant the end of my career, and it was with terrible sadness that I left one of the most rewarding careers anyone could ever have.

CHAPTER 22

Wrestling the Gorilla

Courage is being scared to death and saddling up anyway. —*John Wayne*

A gradual feeling of brokenness settled over me as I came to realize more fully that I truly had a chronic and incurable disease. The realization really took the zest out of the present and the future for me. Slowly I accepted that the disease was not going to go away, and that it would control me. I was frightened to see my body so dysfunctional; the slapping gait, the stiff shoulder, the effects of the medication upon me, the depression, the thoughts of suicide, the insomnia, the dizziness, the nausea, and the detachment. All of these symptoms left me feeling less than human.

I did not realize how seriously affected I was until an incident at the farm. As I was driving my car down the driveway to fill it at the farm gas tank, my foot caught in the space between the accelerator and the brake, and I was too weak to pull my foot back. I very nearly drove the car into the gas tank, which would have exploded and sent me into eternity. I sat there shaking, trying to collect my thoughts, and I asked the Lord, "Why me? What did I do to deserve this end?"

My enthusiasm for life vanished. I was in a tailspin. I tried to see patients in the office, but my shaking hand, my lack of energy, and my detachment left me with a vague and dysfunctional personality that certainly was not therapeutic to my patients. I could sense by the way I was treated that people saw a profound change in my persona. When I looked in the mirror, I saw an old man. Parkinson's has a way of aging you no matter how old you are.

The effects of the medication in some ways were worse than the condition itself. I tried various drug combinations and found myself increasingly unable to focus my attention on the present. The nausea would unbalance me, and constipation made me feel worse. My vision blurred, and my gait was unstable and unbalanced. What was I to do? Where was I to go? Who could I turn to? Kelly was the first to notice the effects of the medication, and she became concerned. I had become totally dependent upon her for driving, dressing myself, and eating, and she assisted me with many other activities of daily living as well. My other family members also expressed their concern, and I realized my condition was affecting not only myself but the whole atmosphere and family climate. The grandchildren would never remember their grandpa without his shaking hand and his shuffling gait.

I went to several different doctors seeking help to manage my condition, but the help I was seeking in the medical profession eluded me. I began to attend a support group for Parkinson's patients, and this is where I found the camaraderie and the hope that turned my life around. I learned that several orthopaedic surgeons in the community had also developed the disease, and as I conferred with them I eventually began to accept that it was indeed possible for me to have this disease. I was eager to hear how they had processed their reactions to the Parkinson's diagnosis. I welcomed and developed a positive attitude. I found these people were marvelously courageous, inspiring, and in control of their condition. Many had managed the disease for between five and ten years, and they continued to be functional. They still had a tremor, but they were walking and coping. This was especially obvious in the young onset patients who, unlike me, still had a lifetime to live, produce, and cope. I was typical of most people with Parkinson's. I had contracted the disease in my mid-sixties, long after I had already made my mark and accomplished my career goals.

Two individuals with PD have greatly influenced me. One woman, Doris, has had Parkinson's disease for fifteen years and yet remains active. She is remarkable. She consistently demonstrates an upbeat attitude; she never appears downhearted or hopeless despite the high incidence of depression in patients with this disease. Her faith is strong, which perhaps explains the overall phenomenon, but the particulars are interesting. When asked about her condition, she responds, "People tell me that I have Parkinson's disease; maybe I do, but as far as I am concerned, I am healed, I have resolved the problem, and I am going on." This mind-set must be one of the reasons she has not deteriorated rapidly over the years.

Another woman who attends the support group is a caregiver whose husband has had Parkinson's disease for fifteen years and is bedridden. She comes to share her experiences and to be encouraged by the energy of the group. Her husband was a physician with a busy practice. When he began to show symptoms and was diagnosed, he was fifty-nine years old. He quit everything, went to bed, and has not moved since. He reportedly has pulled everybody in the family down with him and they suffer greatly. Parkinson's disease affects people differently, but some benefit is to be gained from an aggressive, positive, and upbeat attitude, particularly when it moves one's lifestyle into activity, exercise, and mental challenge.

This group inspired me, and I decided I would attack this condition with all the vigor and enthusiasm I could muster. I read all the articles and information I could find about Parkinson's disease, and I learned that because of its chronic nature and incurability, many treatment regimens were proposed. I decided to find a doctor I could relate to, minimize the medications, improve my diet and nutrition, and pursue exercise with a passion. This I did with the influence of David Zid, a friend who has a thriving business as an athletic trainer and fitness consultant. For ten years, he has frequently come to visit me on the farm. When he can afford the time, he likes to spend a day riding horses with me.

After our trail ride one day, we sat in the barn room talking about my struggle with the disease. He told me he had worked with a number of clients diagnosed with Parkinson's disease and had noticed tremendous improvement in their symptoms when they participated in a regular and consistent exercise program. He believed their amazing results were not so much from the duration or intensity of the exercise as much as the frequency with which they performed the routine. The symptoms especially affected were the capacities for balance, coordination, strength, and general conditioning. He described a number of exercises he had developed that were specific to Parkinson's related problems, including methods to rise from a chair, turn over in bed, get out of bed, and get in and out of an automobile. Several activities improve balance, standing, and initiating the motion of walking. He suggested methods for walking on uneven ground, improving reaction time, strengthening hand grasp, and counteracting tremor. I was immensely interested in his ideas and scheduled a one-on-one training session with him to demonstrate the various exercises. I was amazed that I could actually perform them; I was supposed to be someone with a serious neurologic disease and yet I could exercise and do various activities I previously had thought impossible.

With consistent repetition of the exercise program, I potentially could recondition the neuropathways and anticipate improvement in activity and function.

I was so excited about this prospect that I searched the current medical literature regarding the connection between exercise and Parkinson's symptoms. I was delighted to find some very specific studies that reported exercise has some ongoing degree of benefit for the patient with this disease, depending upon the severity of symptoms and the condition of the patient. A definite correlation between exercise and management of the disease was universally accepted.

My personal exercise agenda had always commenced at five o'clock in the morning. The link between Parkinson's disease and exercise now reinforced my desire to start the day early. First thing in the morning I start with a cardiovascular exercise format. Next I lift weights and perform muscle resistance exercises. Then I have a twenty-minute session where I dance and move quickly around in circles, stretch and bend, perform fine-motor activity, and finally work with the exercise ball. I put together a rigorous daily routine that I performed faithfully.

One day David came to watch my workout and was amazed at my improvements, both in ease of performing the exercises and my flexibility, balance, and coordination in daily activities. After David left, I thought we should write down his program so that other people with Parkinson's disease also could reap the benefits. We commenced to formulate an exercise manual, detailing the specifics of his program in an easy-to-follow format. I am happy to say that this booklet has now been published and is available to Parkinson's patients and their caregivers. Soon I was gaining strength, and I was able to ride my horse and drive my draft horse team.

I found a neurologist who was kind, compassionate, and supportive of my plan, and with her help we regulated the drugs to reduce the side effects. So my enjoyment of the exercise agenda—added to a discovery of oil painting—brought some zest and purpose back into me, and my life began to coalesce. Everything seemed to be improving until an incident occurred one afternoon that really shook the bottom out of my world again.

I was driving my team of horses down the hill from the woods toward the road when the buggy began to slide in the mud. I could not keep the buggy from banging against the backsides of the team of horses, which startled them, and they broke into a full gallop. I could not hold onto the reins because my hands were too weakened from the Parkinson's disease, so I simply put both hands on the handle of the seat and rode out the worst ride of my life. We sped pell-mell through the woods, crashing through low-hanging branches that knocked off my hat and glasses. We were headed straight for a telephone pole. I could do nothing to stop us. When we struck the pole the buggy separated from the horses and I flew from my seat into the wide blue yonder. Luckily I landed on a patch of soft grass. I saw the horses gallop away as the buggy spun circles around the telephone pole. I lay in the grass thinking, "What in the hell is going on? God, what have I done wrong to make such horrible things happen: the Parkinson's, the auto fiasco, and now this?" When I tried to move, my legs stung with pain and my head was spinning. Then I thought, "Oh God, I've broken my neck."

I lay immobile on the ground for what seemed an eternity. Slowly I started to regain movement in my legs and arms, and I worked with them until I could stand up. I felt blood dripping down my face and realized I was bleeding badly from my forehead, but I knew no one would find me out there. So I started walking slowly down the country road toward home. I was about a mile from the farmhouse and continued to walk despite worsening dizziness. As I came to a corner of the field, Kelly happened to be driving by and saw me. She helped me into the car and took me home as I told her what had happened. She examined my wounds and found them all to be superficial. I realized how fortunate I was to have escaped with only minor bruises and abrasions when I could have been more seriously injured, and even killed.

As I recovered over the next couple of days, I was in a sort of psychological suspension. I could not understand why these things were happening. It was as if I had been pulled out of life, and I was witnessing my old life passing by. It really did not seem to matter that I had once been a surgeon, that I had performed thousands of hip replacement operations, that I had developed a successful total hip replacement system, or that I had been chairman of the Ohio State University department of orthopaedics. I was just another human being, suffering, fallen, broken, and depressed.

The days and weeks went by with little change. I was able to ride my horse again, but I sold my team of horses and junked the buggy. I returned to the Parkinson's support group and shared my experience with them. They were sympathetic to my loss but nevertheless encouraged me to be more committed to dealing with my disease in a proactive manner. I took

the cue and returned to my exercise regimen and to painting—as I gradually let go of my love for my profession in orthopaedic surgery.

When life is looked at as an adventure, there is always a new harbor
and a new course ahead. The reality is that if the past was good, so too
will the future be rewarding but perhaps in a different realm. It has been
interesting to see how my attitudes have changed from the initial diagnosis of my disease until now.

I continue to live with the disease, but in a positive way. I continue to
ride my horse, exercise twice a day, eat well, share my experiences with
others, keep my medications to a minimum, and pursue meaningful relationships. I honestly can say that, given another choice with other opportunities, I do not believe I would trade places with anybody. The
experience of being sick and infirm has taught me as much or more about
life and about myself than I learned when I was at the prime of my career.
The humility that comes from suffering is genuine. I see my colleagues,
even those older than I am, who continue to practice in good health. I
used to think how fortunate they are; now I realize that the monotony of
repetitiveness can squelch enjoyment and creativity. How many more hip
replacements can you perform? How many more research papers can you
present?

One of the happy discoveries I made after my Parkinson's diagnosis
was oil painting. I attended an art class with Kelly, mostly out of curiosity, and the teacher asked me if I had ever painted. When I replied that
indeed I never had, she quickly assembled some paint and a canvas and
then handed me a brush. Off I went on this new adventure, and I have
found it most enjoyable. There is for me a freedom of expression in color
and shape and form, and I find I appreciate the opportunity to describe
an impression in either an abstract dimension or a realistic profile. I have
found that painting engenders many of the vibrations I had felt for years
in the operating room. Before me lay an empty canvas to be colored and
shaped, and it would seem similar to the patient who lay on the table,
broken with hip disease, waiting for the implant. As I passed through the
various phases of painting, it was much like preparing myself for medicine. The details and the specifics are similarly rigorous, but the final
expression is aesthetic (see Figures 23, 24).

I brought a certain bias to my painting that has been somewhat limit-
ing to my maturation and development as a serious artist. Oftentimes I
found that I was painting to please my instructor rather than painting to
express what was strictly and completely my own perception. In my opin-

Figure 23.
Still life. Oil painting
by Tom Mallory.

Figure 24. Granddaughter at the beach. Oil painting by Tom
Mallory.

ion, art is utterly subjective. Seldom has it ever been qualified into what is mechanically and technically good art versus what is just splash. This remains an enigma despite the relativism of art (meaning its perception is defined solely by the individual). I decided to paint for myself, to express myself, to dedicate myself to the creative process. I began to paint because I love the color and vibrancy with which the paints blend in a visual aura.

In the pursuit of painting I have adopted the belief that painting is a personal and individual walk; little if anything could be learned by spending hours trying to please an instructor. This philosophy, now that I have completed at least a hundred paintings, has been very fruitful, and I have a constant desire to move on to the next painting. I feel anticipation that I will learn something new every time I paint, and I usually do. It has been very positive and encouraging to find this is true.

I can spend hours painting, and time passes without my being aware of it. I am so captivated by the subject matter and the challenge to bring it into a permanent and lasting dimension. I paint landscapes, mostly, as it is what I feel most comfortable creating. My tremor is almost nonexistent when I am painting. I am so energized, I am not aware of my disease. I am completely absorbed in the art and I feel a sense of relief in having this hobby. The moment I lay down my brush and walk away from the palette, I am reminded again that I have Parkinson's disease. But while I am painting, I am completely oblivious to anything other than expressing what I see before me.

I love to give my paintings to my friends and colleagues even though it is amateur art. It is a personal expression of my affection and respect for the individual. Yet, when I give my paintings away, they are received in many different ways. Some look cross-eyed at the painting and say, "Did you do this?" I nod affirmatively, while they look at me disapprovingly, and I know they did not get the message. Others go wild when they see my art, feeling it is an effort of someone who is sick, to become purposeful and useful in an otherwise deteriorating state. Then there are some who like the painting for the painting's sake. This is the response that I appreciate the most, because these people are the ones I learn from and from whom I glean the greatest contribution.

I sometimes wonder why I ever became a doctor. I missed so many things, and my practice was such an enormous personal sacrifice in terms of time, energy, and effort. Perhaps I could have been an artist or an author, or just a farmer or a horseman. It is all a moot point, now, long gone out of the realm of choice. I have no regrets, just passing thoughts.

Figure 25. Tom Mallory riding with grandson.

Figure 26. Tom and Kelly, the lifelong affair.

This experience of chronic disease has led me into a deeper and more abiding faith in the loving presence of God. I feel as if I am being prepared for heaven because my attitudes are more transcendent and spiritual in dimension. My relationships are more genuine, and I feel a sense of finality and contentment. Although I experience a more rapid progression of the disease now, I feel no despair. I have run the race, finished the course, and am awaiting the call to go up yonder.

Some issues of the disease create concerns that cannot be trivialized, however. My first concern is how I will cope as my condition worsens. Where should I live? And Kelly, how long can she continue to be my caregiver? Will I develop dementia and lose my mind? Will I have to give up my horses? Will I be able to continue to paint? I do not know the answers to these questions, and I do not know that anyone does except the Almighty. But I have one day at a time to go on living, and I am living each day to its fullest. It is with a sense of satisfaction that I continue to live out my days. So when you call me, do not expect me to be at home. I will be exercising, painting, walking, spending time with my family or with other Parkinson's disease patients, or just enjoying my freedom (see Figures 25 and 26).

CHAPTER 23

The Patient, the Doctor, the Lawyer

*Listen to me carefully. Let's proceed with vigor, enthusiasm,
and a sense of optimism.*

What kind of a doctor would I choose to be my physician in the future?
I would be seeking a physician who is not just a good practitioner, a meticulous surgeon, or an expert in the field. I also would need a doctor who
returns telephone calls and displays an awareness of the fundamentals of
medical practice.

As a physician-patient I realized the first thing I had to deal with was
the apprehension and tension coming from the threat that my own physical well-being was in question. As I pondered this, I realized I had just
described the kinds of patients I most appreciated when they came into
my office. Many patients do not realize how their behavior influences the
response of the physicians and the medical staff. Good patients are the
ones who have respect for the physicians and their professional position.
Their expectations are reasonable, they ask good questions, they have a
working knowledge of their symptoms but not authority, they respect
the physicians' time and patient schedules, they display common sense
and appropriate behavior. Physicians beneath their white coats are human
too, and like anyone they love to hear words of appreciation and respect.
If physicians encounter a respectful patient, they are more relaxed, can
think better, are more at ease with their knowledge, and are more perceptive. The appropriate treatment can be prescribed with confidence
when the physicians are allowed to exercise their expertise. When the
fee is charged for a service, good patients understand that it must be
paid. If a problem with finances occurs, they discuss their limitations with

the physicians, and appropriate disclosure is made. When these attitudes and behaviors are followed, the best possible result is achieved.

However, when patients come in with unrealistic expectations or are noncompliant, it becomes very difficult to help them. One of the most difficult events in the doctor-patient relationship is the adversity created when complications occur. And complications will always occur, even when the best care is given, because there is no such thing as zero risk no matter what precautions are taken.

When patients believe and say that they have been mistreated or that malpractice is pending, the whole doctor-patient relationship dissolves and immediately becomes adversarial. To bring a lawsuit against a doctor is a serious course of action. In actuality a lawsuit seldom benefits anyone except the lawyers; the patient usually is unable to enter any kind of relationship financially with the lawyer except for contingency. In the face of a pending lawsuit, the doctor immediately feels threatened, angered, and fearful for his or her business and personal future. Most lawsuits are generated because of a lack of or a break in communication, and from the patient's sense of abandonment. Occasions do arise when wrong has occurred and patients suffer, I do not contest that, but these cases rarely justify the process of litigation. What is the answer then? Perhaps arbitration or mediation, but I do not believe that trial by jury benefits the doctor or the patient.

The question of the capacity of any physician to maintain competence over a lifetime of practice is challenging. As I look back over the thirty years I spent practicing medicine, I see three important aspects of maintaining a physician's positive mind-set: first, a sense of purpose; second, a prevailing optimism; third, continuous and consistent motivation.

First, the sense of purpose of each physician is to promote life, relieve suffering, encourage wellness, and offer comfort in the midst of the insolvable. No greater opportunity exists, I believe, than the mission of the medical profession. The human frame is fraught with many health-related issues that can be addressed and served best by those whose whole heart and soul are in concert with the pathos of the ill and the infirm. This magnificent calling creates the sense of privilege as well as responsibility; the privilege to see the problem and with empathy bring it to solution. This privilege comes with long years of preparation, tendered by experience, but it is always generated by a sense of gratitude for the opportunity to be a doctor of medicine. This purpose never should waver, even in later years when the tendency is to get worn down and worn out.

The second characteristic of a vibrant physician is a positive attitude. I cannot emphasize this too much. It is essential to maintain a positive attitude, in spite of those patients who wear down the physician with complaints or lawsuits, and who drain the emotional vitality out of everyone around them. It is a small percentage of patients who are unrealistic, accusatory, litigious, and adversarial, but these are the ones who do the greatest damage to the physician's attitude. Their behavior can come to dominate the mind and psyche of the physician, to the point that he or she can become reactive or reactionary, defensive, self-protective, reclusive, and distant. These dynamics lead to a feeling of cynicism, to the loss of peace and happiness in life that come from ongoing genuine relationships with others. If a physician falls victim to this mind-set, especially as time passes, he or she will resist making pleasant conversation and will minimize meaningful patient encounters. The practitioner can also take on a feeling of wariness, which can then lead to cynicism, a negative attitude, or a hostile or arrogant reaction to the patient. Cynicism is resisted by choice, one has to choose against it over and over, and unless a physician continually rededicates himself or herself to the original purpose, this trait can be destructive both personally and professionally.

The third characteristic of an effective physician is motivation, or the continued drive to withstand the challenges and responsibilities of the practice of medicine. Sometimes age, illness, or professional fatigue will affect the physician's level of motivation, but taking some time away for introspection can usually help a practitioner return to the fray with vigor, enthusiasm, and a sense of optimism.

CHAPTER 24

Maybe I Was Poisoned

Beware of folly in disguise.

One of the major chemical applications in orthopaedic surgery is the use of methylmethacrylate bone cement for fixation of joint prostheses. The initial and enduring success of total joint replacement is directly related to the use of this cement to affix the metal implant to the skeletal structure. Cement not only creates immediate fixation, but it is durable and thought for the most part to be well tolerated by the human body. One component of the cement is toluene, a known toxin that affects the nervous system. The auditory nervous system seems to be especially susceptible to the effect of toluene, which makes the ear sensitive to environmental noise. When subject to excessive noise, the human ear and neuroauditory system is at heightened risk for damage with progression to the state of deafness.

Orthopaedic surgeons already are at risk for hearing loss because of the continuously noisy work environment of the operating room during joint replacement. Tools such as high-speed drills and power-driven saws create tremendous levels of noise and, over time, have the potential to damage the sense of hearing. Several papers in the scientific research literature have suggested that frequent exposure to high noise levels can cause deafness.

It is not surprising then that the combination of these two phenomena—the neurotoxic toluene exposure from the bone cement and the high levels of noise in the operating room—could explain the early onset deafness I experienced. Moreover, the toluene exposure also may have contributed to my development of Parkinson's disease. Some research suggests it has that potential. The questions remain as to how and why I was affected by these environmental conditions whereas others in the same working conditions have prevailed without impairment. Perhaps I had a predisposition to these problems because both my parents had Parkinson-like symptoms that were never formally diagnosed. Also they were bothered with hearing deficits. Or it may just be a coincidence we are reading too much into because we are always seeking cause-and-effect relationships. Until well-generated clinical data can be established and a direct relationship can be drawn, the association and the results remain speculative. However, the possibility that it might be correlated does raise an interesting question.

Had I known the potential dangers, what would I have done differently? I still would have had to mix the cement to insert the prosthesis into the patient, and I still would have had to use the noisy power instruments. I am sure effective protective mechanisms might be utilized to protect a surgeon from these effects. However, even if I had been protected from these particular risks, other risks probably would have arisen. We live in a world where there is no zero risk, so one must be somewhat cautious. There are, however, overriding attitudes that make risk tolerable even if the consequences are malevolent. At the time I was choosing a profession, I was young and I felt invincible. Even the known risk would not have prevented me from pursuing the passion I felt for this operation. I had to spend my life doing something, and I cannot think of a better cause than helping the broken and the hurting, the sick and the dying, as a physician and a surgeon. I have taken the risk and incurred the consequences, and now I sit in a state of infirmity. The fires are still burning in my spirit and soul for my profession, but my body is weak and fragile, disoriented and dysfunctional.

What a wide bridge exists between what was and what is! I am not so sure you can live a prophylactic life, for we know so little of what the future holds. The question remains when one reaches this state of lesser health, does life still hold meaning, purpose, passion, and anticipation? The physical strength, the quickness, and the agility of this athlete all are gone, but a peace of mind has replaced those attributes when I realize I was in the game of life, fully committed, living through the peaks and valleys onward to an eternal existence. There was a time when I feared no person, situation, or encounter. My mind-set was completely oblivious, purely adventurous, with no sense of risk. I did things simply to experience the effect at any cost. It was during those periods of my life that I made some quite meaningful contributions. So if I have been poisoned by methylmethacrylate and the noisy operating room, I must tell others to beware lest they too be poisoned.

Then I wonder, what were some of the other poisons in my life? This may sound strange, but I think the activity frenzy was one of the most damaging of the poisons. I pushed a busy scheduled chaos throughout my life. Although I was reasonably well organized, I often felt overwhelmed and failed in any attempt to identify the essentials. Doing more did not necessarily make my life better. "Better" came to mean balance. However, this balance was elusive. The state of balance is subject to attitudes of good fortune, popularity, peer recognition, family, and children's success. Therefore, perhaps the pursuit of balance is a poison in a sense.

Gluttony is another poison, and it has many faces. There is the gluttony of basic deprivation and hard work, sweat and sacrifice. I succumbed to these elements when I pursued marathon running. Gluttony can be an accumulation of clutter and possessions that stifles your time and resources. Gluttony can be an indulgence in food and drink, pleasure, sensual and other stimulation. Gluttony can be a desire for recognition, craving acceptance and acknowledgment. However, of all the poisons that are most devastating to the physician, the greatest is the indulgence of cynicism. Often I have encountered medical students who are optimistic about the future of their careers and their professional lives, and then, when I encountered them later in life during their journey as a physician, I find they have lost the passion and love for the patient, the curiosity for the phenomenon they are preserving, and the desire to help the suffering.

I remember vividly the time I visited my vascular surgery professor when he was dying of cancer. It made me sad to think that he was in the prime of his career, a kind and gentle man, with the fully developed qualities of a mature and outstanding physician and surgeon. I had the utmost respect for this man. Now as I consider how disease ended my career, I realize that really there is nothing to be sad about, no reason to be cynical; the poisons have their antidotes. Although there are many poisons in life, they need not be fatal. On to the future, show me the road ahead!

CHAPTER 25

Life Comes Bearing Gifts

Pursuing a career in medicine creates a sense of a spiritual journey. This is especially true when a physician is willing to examine his or her beliefs concerning human suffering in the light of what is good and proper. Moreover, it is important to explore one's desire, prejudice, bias, pride, even emotion as it relates to the mind-set one brings to the doctor-patient relationship.

Indeed one must have a brave soul to question one's destiny. As a little boy I went to Sunday school class at the Methodist church and sang "Jesus Loves Me." I felt good in my perception of a supernatural presence. My feelings remained nondescript until I was in high school and I began to consider the origin of humanity and to contemplate the destiny of humankind. These issues were provoked in my mind by discussions with my father, who realized that there was both a moral order in the universe and a design that indicated a supreme being. For me the purpose in life was to do something productive, and medicine fit the bill.

At the university I had many discussions regarding theological and spiritual issues, and at one time I even thought I might be a pastor. I met some evangelical Christians who talked about being born again. I remember the day Martin Luther King came to Miami University to talk about the issues of segregation and civil rights. "Now there is a godly man," I said to myself. He seemed virtuous, pure, and committed to a profound sense of morality. He seemed the kind of person I should strive to be. I attended church occasionally, when it was convenient, but the whole religious experience seemed relatively unimportant.

I think one of the most moving experiences of my life was when I looked into the face of my first newborn son, Scott. I realized that something very special had occurred, and it was an act of God's benevolence.

Kelly and I together had created a new life, and a spiritual bond existed between father, mother, and child. It indeed was supernatural.

On a trip to England with several of my colleagues, we came upon a large sign outside Charnley's hip center that spelled "Reserved Prof. Charnley." When I saw the sign, I fell down on the ground, grasped my hands, and bowed before the sign. I did it in a joking manner and my colleagues got a big chuckle out of it. But Charnley was indeed one of my gods; I admired everything he did and said and was, and I bought into his philosophy 100 percent just as I had done with Otto Aufranc. In my mind these men were superdocs, and they became my idols. I satisfied my spiritual yearnings for significant meaning independent of a universal and holy God. I was full of raw ambition with driving determination. I was going to take this technology and go as far as I could go with it. In doing so, I would be virtuous and contribute to the world, making it a little better every day. This was my religion for the moment.

One Saturday the phone rang. It was my brother David. He said his little girl had just been run over by a car. She was dead. I staggered back with the phone still in my hand. I could not imagine anything so terrible happening. This little girl was so cute, so pretty, so precious, so full of life. How could God allow such a thing to happen? I got into the car with Kelly and we drove to my brother's house. The next several days were a living nightmare as together we buried their little girl. I embraced my brother and sister-in-law and saw the hurt and brokenness in their blurry eyes. I felt very badly for them and was preoccupied with the question of what the whole episode meant. I was distraught for many days. Why did this happen? What did it mean? How could I help my brother with his suffering? Would the hurt ever go away?

One October morning as I drove out of the driveway in a new Mercedes and wearing a newly tailored suit, I was struck by the beauty of the morning. The moon hung low, the sky was clear, and the dawn was coming. The corn was golden in its ripening state, the air was crisp. I was overwhelmed with a sense of gratitude to God for giving me such a wonderful life. However, for the first time in my life, on that morning, I felt a profound sense of accountability toward God. This created a sense of impending fear and anxiety that I really did not want to tell anyone about.

I began to study the Bible diligently. God was defined as sovereign, almighty, powerful, creator, designer, but most interestingly as a person. He had created man and woman for a relationship with Him. The purpose of life is to know God and to enjoy Him forever. Mankind has fallen from grace and therefore has an eventual accountability that can be corrected only by believing in the deity of Christ and His work of redemption.

I could see the validity in this perception, but I did not want to become a religious freak. My basic logic had always been, show it to me and I will believe. However, God requires one to believe before it becomes obvious. I took a leap of faith, now I believe, and I am convinced. This belief has had a very stabilizing effect on me and has produced a continued sense of well-being. Now that I am caught in the process of aging and I suffer from an incurable disease, I understand that even time and circumstance cannot shatter love and hope. As my faith has deepened I have experienced an increase in the presence of peace. My faith generates benevolence in friendships, it enriches my memory, stimulates my courage, and matures my soul.

As I reflect on my many encounters with physicians, I am amazed at how few have developed a personal faith. They commit what one might call soul suicide. They squash their spirituality, they fear their emotions, and they come to a state of cynicism and despair. They live in fear of their own impending mortality. They are bothered with loneliness and have a sense of despair, not only in their personal lives but also as physicians. Despite the fact that they are practicing a profession with deep and profound purpose, they seldom enjoy the spiritual benefits of the practice of medicine. They have a difficult time handling the issues of morality and character; they lack the virtues of modesty and civility. The most pathetic part of spiritually starved physicians is their loss of the capacity to believe, which is a sorry legacy considering such a noble profession.

Life is ever renewing. My sons' marriages produced a flock of grandchildren with a male prominence. Most of my grandchildren were born after I was diagnosed with Parkinson's disease, so their memories of their grandfather will always be of my shaking, feeble, stooped physical profile. However, when I interact with them, they find no wimp. Although I do not have the strength and stamina I once had, my encounters with them are fulfilling, and I do not allow much to pass me by. I always encourage them to have fun, but our time together is always wrapped in a message of serious engagement. My goals for my grandchildren have not changed from those I had for my own children, and I am pleased when I see their parents encouraging them to be responsible and respectable citizens.

The farm is a beautiful place for the grandchildren. They romp and roam the hillsides with keen expectation. The winters are thrilling, with slopes of snow for sledding and room to play for hours in the cold, stimulating climate. In the summers, the children roam the farm on trails, sometimes on horseback or motorized dirt bikes, but often with their parents or grandparents.

The Fourth of July is a particularly exciting day when all the family gathers and celebrates the day with food and festivities. The games we play are competitive and are always rewarded with acknowledgment of merit and accomplishment. As I look out over the polo field and see the children playing, I realize that life has been a series of seasons. Oh, that I may play this season as well as I have tried in other times. Perhaps my physical impairment is meant to emphasize a focus on stimulating, challenging, loving, and accepting my grandchildren.

Because the majority of them are male, I will focus on manliness, which I consider essential for their rearing. Responsibility is born from the awareness to protect, preserve, cherish, and care. Cultivating new and fresh ideas, seeking adventures that challenge, to dare, to risk, to build, to accomplish and achieve, this is the essence of manliness. This produces a man who knows his history and his past, respects the family name, and encourages virtue. Manliness further expresses itself with the love of sports, the ruggedness that comes from outdoor living, and the keen sense of competition.

How does this relate to my grandchildren? I hope that one or more will feel the call to the medical profession and they will share the Mallory legacy. The practitioner of medicine is only as strong as his or her individual character, which brings me back to my sphere of influence. The lessons I learned of character building began a long way from the operating room and the lecture circuit. They were encountered in other ways, even on the college campus, in patient encounters, from dangerous surgery, frivolous and serious lawsuits, and all the other things that echo in my past.

My world has changed, now the stadium is empty, the crowds have gone home. Now, sitting in my chair, I see a little guy with questions such as "What did you do, Grandpa, when you used to work? Grandpa, why does your hand shake all the time? Grandpa, why do you like horses so much? Grandpa, who is Jesus? Grandpa, can I have another chocolate chip cookie?" I cherish this new audience. For me, now, being a good grandparent is the essence of virtue. This is perhaps one of the most challenging times of my life. I am more history and legacy than I am actual reality. My physical impairments construct a barrier that allows me to translate myself to a more distant influence, which is less intense, less judgmental, less expecting, but nevertheless curious and continuing.

It is as if I am a spectator, watching the games everyone is playing, making certain the boundaries are not violated and the culture is wholesome and appropriate. My attitude is one of gratitude and abiding appreciation for God's benevolence toward my family. No longer a physician, no longer an orthopaedic surgeon, no longer a professional person, I find these distant memories are fading. Present realities have replaced them and are consuming my time and thought as I enjoy the present. Life is indeed good in all seasons.

This evening is a warm summer's night, and some passing, concluding thoughts occur as I sit on the porch looking out over the woods and meadows that grace my farm. My thoughts wander back to days gone by. So many unusual things have happened that my life and its events cannot be considered random. I firmly believe that providence played the greater part. But I can see now that I have completed the cycle. I have made the loop; in a sense I am where I started so many years ago. The only difference is that now I am not ambitious. Most of the things I thought were meaningful then have been experienced, encountered, or appreciated. I ran the race because the personal characteristics of my youth were unbridled energy and determination. At times this ambitious drive to succeed was a hindrance, but most times it fueled the fire within me. Without it I never would have been the Chief.

I leave the profession now to those who follow after me, who can serve the needs and treat the suffering and pain of countless people with arthritis and other musculoskeletal conditions. I spent my life looking for keys; when I unlocked one door, it led to another door, and when I found its key, I was on to the next. I'm living a fulfilling life even in a failing body. I see no reason for cynicism, doubt, or despair. I do not allow to take root in my mind any thoughts that might lead to depression. For myself I have determined that depression, the modern-day mental illness, is a self-centered mind-set; it is seldom provoked but is tolerated as an attitude. It promotes preoccupation with self, and its effects can be reversed promptly when one considers others first. I attempt to capture depressing thoughts and reverse them; this reversal encompasses a fundamental sense of gratitude for what already has come to pass, and for the unshakable confidence in the present and the future, that life is an episode and not a condition.

I often ask myself, what were my happiest days? Becoming a physician was an extremely rewarding experience during my lifetime, but it unfortunately may have stifled other areas of my life. I now have a conditional

Figure 27. Doug Brewer, PA, the Chief, and Adolph Lombardi Jr.

response that says every day of my life has the potential for happiness if the right attitudes prevail. During my final years, I am left to reflect that the view was worth the climb up the mountain. Time and circumstance have been a thief; they stole my awareness of time, left me believing that I always would be a physician.

I never quite understood why they called me Chief, maybe it is because the world always wants a leader or a hit person, someone to forge the way. The circle now has come full circle, and I am complete just being who I am. Who I was is covered in this book, and when I was doing all those things, I guess I was the Chief (see Figure 27). But now my life moves on to the future. Who I will be remains in God's hands, but what I do know is that I will be devoid of titles, achievements, possessions, family, and accomplishments. As I sit in my rocking chair on the porch, musing on the journey I have undertaken throughout my life, I am filled with gratitude for the experiences that were mine, the relationships I built, the satisfaction of helping thousands of people live more comfortably, and the privilege to reflect now on the true blessings of life.

Ecclesiastes 12
Honor and enjoy your creator while you are still young.
Before the years take their toll, and your vigor wanes.
Before your vision dims and the world blurs.
And the winter years keep you close to the fire.

Life, lovely while it lasts, is soon over.
Life as we know it, precious and beautiful, ends.
The body is put back into the same ground it came from.
The spirit returns to God, who first breathed it.

The words of the wise prod us to live well.
They are like nails hammered home, holding life together.
They are given by God, the one Shepherd.

Taken from *The Message: The Bible in Contemporary Language,* by Eugene H. Peterson.